THE PRACTICAL BOOK OF
PICTURE FRAMING

THE PRACTICAL BOOK OF
PICTURE FRAMING

How to make more than 100 classic and decorative frames

Rian Kanduth

southwater

This edition is published by Southwater,
an imprint of Anness Publishing Ltd,
Blaby Road, Wigston,
Leicestershire LE18 4SE;
info@anness.com

www.southwaterbooks.com; www.annesspublishing.com

If you like the images in this book and would like to investigate using them for
publishing, promotions or advertising, please visit our website
www.practicalpictures.com for more information.

A CIP catalogue record for this book is available from the British Library.

Publisher Joanna Lorenz
Project Editor Simona Hill
Copy Editors Beverley Jollands and Heather Haynes
Designer Nigel Partridge
Production Controller Mai-Ling Collyer

PUBLISHER'S NOTES
Protective clothing should be worn when performing some of the tasks described
in this book. Wear rubber (latex) gloves for grouting and using glass etching paste;
wear protective gloves and goggles when cutting glass, breaking mosaic tesserae with a
hammer or tile nippers, or cutting wire or sheet metal. Wear a face mask when sawing,
sanding or drilling MDF, working with powdered grout or using solvent-based sprays.

Every effort has been made to ensure the project instructions are accurate. The author
and publisher cannot accept liability for any resulting damage or loss to persons or
property as a result of carrying out any of the projects. Before you begin any project
you should be sure and confident that you understand the instructions.

Contents

Introduction

Framing pictures, photographs and mirrors is a creative, absorbing and ultimately very satisfying craft. It requires a meticulous, careful approach and takes time and practice, but your efforts will be well rewarded by the pride and pleasure you will feel in a job well done. As well as explaining all the different techniques involved in framing pictures and textiles, this book contains 100 step-by-step projects, ranging from small to large, and from easy to challenging.

The first chapter explains how to make a basic frame and mount (mat), before moving on to more ambitious styles including multiple-window frames and box frames. The rest of the book helps you to build on these basic skills, using a variety of different materials. You can learn how to decorate frames with paint and colour,

how to make frames using paper, cardboard, wire and tin, how to embellish them with fabric, flowers and beads, and, finally, how to extend your frame-making skills using clay and mosaic. Follow the symbols to gauge the complexity of the projects. The

simplest, marked with a single symbol, are those that a complete beginner could tackle; five symbols indicate that an advanced level of skill is needed.

There are frames to suit everyone, from funky to traditional, from rustic and naive to modern and

minimalist. Some are embellished with mosaic and beads; others use gilding, lead or wire to add designer style. Sometimes the simplest styles create the most striking effects, but they should always suit the image they are framing. That needn't be an

original painting – everything from leaves to family snaps can be creatively displayed and will look brilliant if you put it in a fantastic frame.

If you are unsure about a particular technique, practise first on scrap paper, cardboard, wood or fabric – none of the materials used in framing are very expensive. Once you feel confident with the techniques, you can adapt the projects to suit your

own style and interior. Above all, have fun making wonderful, unique frames for yourself and your friends and family.

The Art of
Framing

The ideal frame is one that effectively shows off the picture within it, whether that is a work of art, a photograph or the reflection in a mirror. It should not overpower the image, or clash with its style. Careful choice is one of the most important skills in framing, and knowing what will work best is something that often comes with practice. This chapter aims to show you how to take everything into account and frame your pictures successfully.

Framing Facts

Although it may seem daunting to begin with, framing is actually not really difficult once you have decided on the style of your frame and worked out the materials you are going to use. Invest in the right tools and equipment from the start: they'll make framing easy and enjoyable and ensure that you produce results you are proud to hang on your walls. Although items like a mitre saw and clamp may seem expensive, they are essential for perfect mitring and will enable you to achieve the absolute accuracy you need for a professional-looking result.

This chapter sets out all the basics of framing. If you are a complete novice, it's sensible to read through all the instructions and advice carefully before you begin. Even if you think you already know your way around a picture frame, you'll find useful tips to help you refine your technique. The chapter begins with mounts (mats) – which can be just as important as a frame in making the most of a picture. Once you have learned how to make a basic mount, you can master the art of

making a stepped-window mount, multiple-window mounts for a set of pictures, a fabric mount and even shaped-window mounts. There are also some tips and ideas for effective ways to decorate a mount to show off a picture to its best effect.

Then there are step-by-step instructions for making the actual frames, from the basic shapes to the more unusual. Detailed illustrations show how to saw mitred corners, how to assemble a frame, and how to make the most of mouldings. You can also

learn how to create an unusual jigsaw-style frame, a multiple-window frame, a box frame, a cross-over frame and even a frame constructed from rustic

driftwood. The art of glass-cutting is illustrated, with advice on the type of glass to use.

Finally, there are projects showing how to frame different sorts of pictures, whether they are oils on canvas, three-dimensional objects or even engraved stone, with some hints on hanging and fixtures. Armed with all this information, you can set about filling your walls with beautiful framed pictures.

Most of the items listed below are basic frame-making equipment, which you will use many times, so it is worth investing in any you do not already have. Specialist tools are available from framing suppliers.

Materials and Equipment

is a metal fixture, usually bolted to a workbench, in which moulding lengths are cut at a 45° angle.

Corner gauge

When decorating mounts (mats), this fits into the corner of the window to allow pencil corner marks to be positioned accurately.

Craft knife

This has multiple uses in picture framing. There are several varieties so choose one that feels comfortable.

Cutting mat

Essential when cutting with a craft knife, as it protects the underlying surface. Self-healing cutting mats stay smooth and free from score marks.

Drill and drill bits

Both electric and hand drills are suitable for frame making.

D-rings

Picture wire is threaded through these for hanging. D-rings are available as single or double. Attach them to the backing board with butterflies (rivet-like fixings), or screw into the back of the frame.

Frame clamp

Frames are clamped to hold the joints together while the glue dries.

Acid-free hinging tape

Water-soluble gummed tissue tape is used to make tab hinges to secure artwork to a backing board. It should be weaker than the paper of the artwork so that it tears first if the assembly is broken up.

Blade

When cutting windows in mounts (mats) a blade is needed to release the cut corners to avoid tearing and give a neat, sharp finish.

Bradawl (awl)

Used for making initial holes in hardboard or wood.

Burnishing tools

A burnishing bone is for smoothing the cut edges of a mount (mat). The traditional gilder's agate burnisher is used to polish water-gilded surfaces.

Clamps

These come in all shapes and sizes and have various uses. A mitre clamp

Framer's point gun

This specialist tool is used for fitting up picture frames. It inserts flat pins horizontally into the moulding to hold the backing board in place.

Glass cutter

Diamond-headed and tungsten types for heavy-duty glass cutting can be quite expensive, but cheaper alternatives are available for domestic use.

Glue

PVA (white) glue is used to hold the mitre joints in frames. Two-part **epoxy resin glue** forms a very strong bond for joining metal and stone. **Rubber solution glue** is used for attaching fabrics to mounts (mats).

Hacksaw

Used in a mitre clamp to cut wooden or manufactured mouldings. There are various types of blade, including blades for cutting metal mouldings.

Heatgun

Normally intended for stripping painted wood, an electric heat gun can be used to scorch patterns in wooden mouldings.

Mitre box

This two-sided wooden box has deep slots at a 45° angle to take a tenon saw for cutting moulding lengths. Its high sides keep the saw vertical and help to steady the moulding.

Mount (mat) board

The wide range of mount boards available fall mainly into two categories: regular and conservation.

Regular boards are cheaper but the acid from the wood pulp used to make them will damage artwork over the years. Conservation boards are acid-free and will not damage artwork.

Mount (mat) cutter

A tool for cutting a bevelled window out of mount (mat) board. You can buy hand-held versions from good art stores and framing suppliers.

Paintbrushes

Use flat-face oil and sable brushes, approximately 1cm/½in and 2.5cm/1in wide, for detailing and pointing. Use stencil brushes for stencilling.

Panel pins (brads)

Thin pins are used for joining frames and tacking the backing board to the frame in the final assembly stage.

Safety gloves

Wear rubber (latex) gloves when painting, and protective cotton or leather gloves when handling metal foils or cutting glass.

Safety mask

Use with any paint or varnish sprays to avoid inhaling the mist, and when sawing MDF, which creates a large amount of fine dust.

Straight edge rule

Use for marking and cutting lines.

Tack hammer

A lightweight hammer is used for tapping in panel pins (brads); it can be used as an alternative to the V-nail joiner when assembling frames.

Tape measure

Used for measuring artwork, mounts and moulding.

Tenon saw

A 30cm/12in-wide flat saw used with a mitre box to cut wooden or manufactured mouldings. The reinforced upper edge keeps the blade rigid to allow very accurate straight cuts.

T-square

A measuring tool used to give a true square or rectangle. Used for marking up mounts (mats) and cutting glass.

V-nail joiner

When the frame is being joined together it is used to push V-shaped nails across the mitres to hold them together. It can also be used to secure the backing board to the frame.

V-nails

Used with the V-nail joiner to underpin the frame.

Wire cutters

Used to cut picture wire.

Wood

Mouldings are available in both soft and hardwoods in many designs. Those sold for framing have a ready-cut rebate to take the picture and glass. **Plywood** is an ideal material for making frames. It consists of thin sheets of wood glued together; the grains of wood in adjacent sheets are arranged at right angles to each other, which makes it exceptionally strong. It can be used to make backing boards as an alternative to **hardboard**.

A picture frame serves a dual purpose: it is designed both to display and to protect the painting or photograph within it, and all its various components contribute to these functions.

The Parts of a Frame

The component parts of the frame form a multi-layered sandwich, with the picture or photograph as the filling. The backing board, which is usually made of hardboard, gives rigidity. If delicate artwork is being framed, the backing board should be overlaid by an acid-free barrier to give extra protection. The image itself can be secured to the backing board using tab hinges of acid-free paper tape.

When a picture is to be displayed within a window mount (mat), it is customary to allow a slightly larger margin at the bottom of the mount than at the top or sides, to correct an optical illusion which occurs when the picture is hung on the wall. If all the margins were the same width, the bottom one would appear smaller than the others.

It is very important to take precise measurements before making a mount, and it is usually worth checking all your measurements before you begin to cut anything.

If a mount is not used, narrow wooden fillets should be inserted in the frame between the glass and the picture, to prevent the glass from touching the surface of the artwork. These will be visible when the picture is hung, so the wood should be selected to coordinate well with the image and the frame.

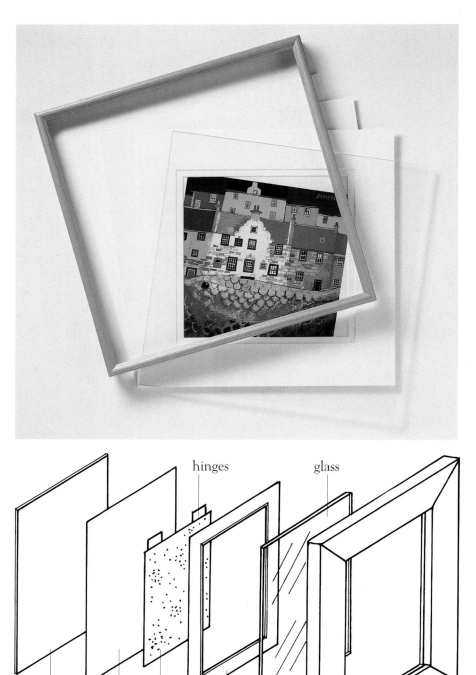

backing board

barrier

hinges

artwork

mount (mat) board

glass

frame

The mount (mat) keeps the artwork away from the glass. Paper expands and contracts with temperature and humidity changes, which can result in buckling. The mount allows room for movement in the artwork.

Single Window Mount

you will need

picture

mount (mat) board

tape measure

soft pencil

ruler

straight edge

mount (mat) cutter

cutting mat

blade

eraser

acid-free hinging tape

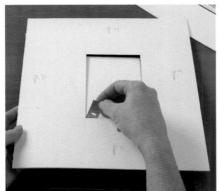

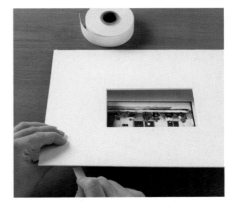

1 Measure the picture vertically and horizontally and add 7.5cm/3in to the top and both sides and 9cm/3½in at the bottom. You can now use these dimensions to cut the mount (mat) board to size.

2 Mark the inner measurements on the reverse side of the mount board using a pencil and ruler. Join up the pencil marks, crossing the lines so that you can see clearly where you need to stop cutting.

3 Line up the straight edge against the first marked line, push the mount cutter blade into the board and move it steadily along the marked line to cut out the window. Go over the pencil mark cross-overs only slightly, to avoid visible cross-cuts on the face of the mount.

4 Cut the other three sides, turning the board so that you are always cutting vertically. Once you have cut out the window, carefully insert a blade into each corner and trim the edge to release the centre freely. This will avoid any tearing of the corners. Erase the pencil marks.

5 Place the window mount face up on the picture below it, and line them up. Attach the picture to the mount using acid-free hinging tape on the top edge of the artwork.

Use multiple-window mounts (mats) for collections of photographs or memorabilia that have a common theme, such as a series of old sepia prints, photographs of family members or a set of architectural studies.

Multiple-window Mount

you will need

pictures

mount (mat) board

soft pencil

ruler

T-square

mount (mat) cutter

cutting mat

blade

eraser

acid-free hinging tape

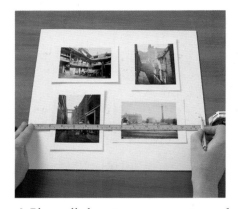

1 Place all the pictures on a piece of mount (mat) board. Using a ruler and pencil, mark the horizontal measurements of the two top and bottom pictures, just touching the pictures on all sides with the pencil.

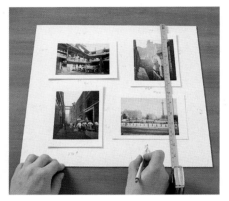

2 Next, mark the vertical measurements of the top and bottom pictures in pencil, again just touching the pictures on all sides.

3 Once the measurements have been marked, join them up using a pencil and a ruler. Be sure to make crossovers, so when cutting the mount you will know where to stop.

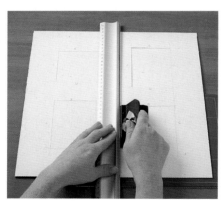

4 Cut out all the windows, cutting the left-hand side of each first, then the top, then the right-hand side, then the bottom. Move the mount board as you work, so you are cutting vertically. Erase the pencil marks.

5 When all the windows have been cut, position and hinge the pictures as for the single window mount.

This design is similar to a single window mount (mat) but with the addition of a second mount, with a slightly larger window opening, stuck on top. This results in an interesting stepped look.

Stepped Mount

you will need
tape measure
mount (mat) cutter
straight edge
cutting mat
2 pieces of mount (mat) board
soft pencil
T-square
blade
eraser
PVA (white) glue
glue brush

1 Measure the picture to be framed vertically and horizontally. Following the measurements, cut two pieces of mount (mat) board the same size, in proportion with the picture.

2 Mark the dimensions of the picture on both boards in the desired position. On one piece, draw a second line 1cm/½in larger than the original measurement on each side.

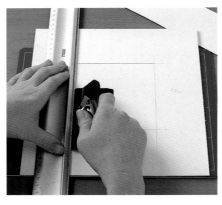

3 Cut the small windows from one board and the larger window from the second board using a mount (mat) cutter and blade and protecting the work surface with a cutting mat.

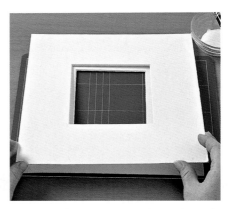

4 Erase the pencil marks and apply PVA (white) glue to the back of the larger window mount. Place this on the face of the other mount and press down well to ensure good adhesion.

Covering a mount (mat) with fabric adds richness and depth to a background, especially if you use a luxury fabric such as silk or velvet. Traditionally, Persian and Indian textiles were framed in a fabric mount.

Fabric-covered Mount

you will need

pre-cut mount (mat)
fabric
cutting mat
tape measure
craft knife
ruler
fabric glue
glue brush
ink roller

1 Place the pre-cut mount (mat) face down on the fabric, on a cutting mat. Cut out the fabric 2.5cm/1in larger all around to allow for overlaps. Trim the corners of the fabric to make folding over easier.

2 Apply a thin, even coat of fabric glue to the face of the mount. Centre the fabric on top of the mount, press down and rub gently with a clean ink roller to ensure good adhesion.

3 Turn over the covered mount so that the fabric is face down. Cut out the window, leaving a 2.5cm/1in border of fabric for the overlaps.

4 Cut mitres in the overlap fabric in the window. Apply fabric glue to the mount where the overlaps will lie, then fold over the fabric edges and press down firmly.

5 Fold down the overlaps on the side edges of the mount. At the corners, hold the fabric firmly and cut a mitre with a craft knife, then apply fabric glue and press the fabric down.

Mounts (mats) with a curved edge can be cut using a special bevel mount cutter. The curve can be cut freehand following a line or around a template in the shape and size required.

Shaped Mounts

Round mount It is possible to cut around a saucer or plate to make a circular window, although this method limits the size of the frame you can use.

you will need

mount (mat) board cut to fit frame
2 pieces of scrap mount board
ruler
pencil
template
bevel mount (mat) cutter
map pins
straight edge

Below: Shaped mounts look effective around small subjects such as portrait miniatures or studies of single flowers.

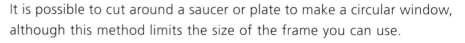

 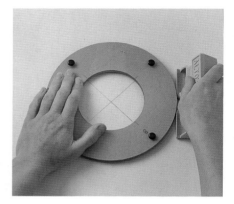

1 Place the mount (mat) board right side up on top of two pieces of scrap board to protect the work surface. Position a ruler diagonally across the corners and mark the centre. Pin the template to the board centred on the pencil mark.

2 Place the cutter next to the template. Push the cutter forward and down until the blade is in the mount board and the bottom of the cutter is flat. Cut a quarter of the way around the template, keeping the contact points on the cutter flush with the template and the cutter flat.

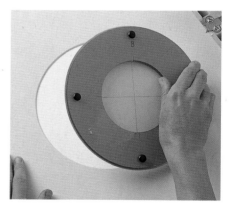

3 Leave the cutter in place and rotate the three layers of board a quarter-turn. Cut another quarter and rotate again. Repeat all the way around. Lift out the template and window.

Combination mount — This interesting shape resembles an arched window and is made using a round template at the top of a rectangular opening.

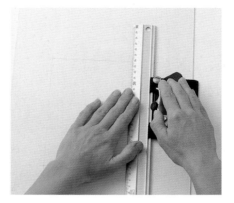

1 Measure the picture horizontally and vertically. Add 6cm/2¼in to the sides and the top, and 6.5cm/2½ in to the bottom. Following these measurements, cut the mount (mat) board to size and draw the shape on the reverse side. Tuck two pieces of scrap mount board underneath.

2 Line up the straight edge on the outside of the marked line. Push the mount cutter into the board just beyond the crossover point and move steadily along the line to just beyond the crossover point at the other end. Cut the remaining sides.

3 Turn the mount over and fit the window scrap back in position. Mark the centre point of the circle template on the right side and pin in position. Cut around the template.

Oval mount — An oval template can be drawn and, with practice, cut freehand. This method makes an oval to an exact width and height.

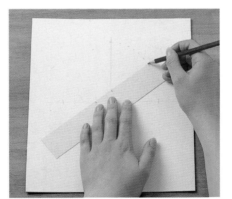

3 Mark the board then move the strip about 9mm/⅜in round, keeping the centre marks on the horizontal and vertical lines, and mark the board again. Keep moving the strip round until the first quarter is complete. Repeat to complete each quarter in turn until the oval is finished.

1 Determine the size of oval required. Divide the mount (mat) board vertically and horizontally with two pencil lines at right angles to each other. Mark the length and width of the oval on the lines.

2 Place a strip of thin cardboard on the horizontal line and mark the centre and width of the oval. Turn the strip vertically and place the width point on the height point. Mark the new centre position on the strip. Place the strip across the two axes near the vertical, aligning the two centre marks with the two axis lines.

4 Tuck a couple of pieces of scrap mount board under the marked oval. Insert map pins inside the oval to secure the layers. Use a mount cutter freehand to cut along the line. Leave the cutter in the mount board and turn the boards as you cut each quarter, taking care to join the two ends of the cut neatly.

Window mounts (mats) can be decorated in lots of different ways. Decorative papers, ruled lines, washes and marbling add extra richness around the aperture and will complement and enhance the picture.

Decorating a Mount

Marbled border

you will need

pre-cut mount (mat)

soft pencil

ruler or straight edge

decorative paper

cutting mat

craft knife

spray adhesive or PVA (white) glue

The subtle colour combinations of marbled or other decorated paper make a pretty border for a delicate sketch or painting.

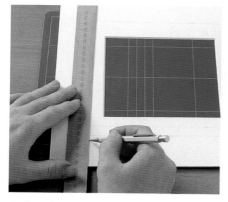

1 On the face of the pre-cut mount (mat), mark out light lines with a pencil and ruler or straight edge, setting out where the decorative border is to be placed. Place the decorative paper on a cutting mat to protect the surface. Using a craft knife and ruler, measure and cut the paper into appropriate-sized strips.

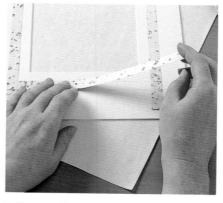

2 Spray adhesive on the reverse of the strips and stick them along the lines.

3 Using a ruler and craft knife, mitre each corner. Remove the spare paper.

Decorative lines

Lines are normally drawn in gold or a soft shade such as grey or sepia. Single lines are usually drawn between 5–15mm/¼–⅝in away from the bevel. Double lines usually have a 3–5mm/⅛–¼in gap between them.

you will need

corner gauge

pencil

pre-cut mount (mat)

lining ink

distilled water

lining pen

scrap mount (mat) board

small watercolour brush

bevelled ruler

eraser

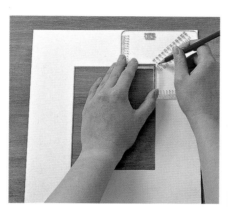

1 Use a corner gauge to mark the position of the lines lightly on the mount (mat) with a sharp pencil. Dilute the lining ink to the required shade with distilled water (tap water can leave brown marks as it dries). Test the colour on a piece of scrap board.

2 Adjust the prongs of the lining pen to the required width. Load the pen with ink using a small watercolour brush. You need enough to complete the line but not so much that the ink comes out in a blob.

3 Draw the line between the dots using a ruler with a bevel edge to prevent the ink bleeding. Turn the mount round and draw the remaining lines. Once the ink has dried, the pencil marks can be erased without damaging the lines.

Colourwashing

Watercolour paint can be diluted with distilled water to create a very pale wash.

To add more colour around a mount (mat), paint in a light wash between two ink lines. Use a brush that is the exact width of the gap. Mix distilled water with watercolour paint to make a very pale wash. Paint on a wash of clear water first to delay the drying process, then brush the colour between the lines.

Below: A selection of decorative effects to enhance the artwork displayed.

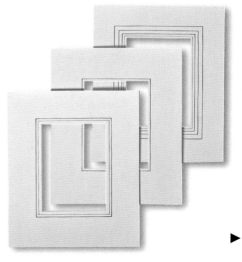

Sponging

Sponging is a quick and easy way to decorate a mount (mat). Use a combination of pale colours that blend well together, then outline them with a fine line to provide definition.

you will need

pencil

corner gauge

pre-cut mount (mat)

magic tape

ruler

craft knife

acrylic paint

palette or plate

natural sponge

paper towels

lining ink

lining pen

bevelled ruler

1 Using a sharp pencil and corner gauge, mark the position of the lines and area to be sponged on the mount (mat). Stick lengths of magic tape outside the marks on the corners of the mount to blank off the area to be decorated. Using a ruler and craft knife, cut the tape flush at the corners.

2 Mix the paint colours required. Dip the sponge in the first colour and remove the excess on a paper towel. Gently dab the sponge between the pieces of magic tape.

3 Wash the sponge and dry it by squeezing it out in a paper towel. Apply a second colour with the sponge to achieve the desired effect. Allow the paint to dry and then carefully peel off the magic tape.

4 Draw lines in a toning colour on each side of the sponging. To avoid smudging the ink, draw all the inside lines first, turning the mount around for each line, and then complete the outside lines.

Successful framing is all about choosing a mount (mat) and frame that suits the image and takes into account where it will hang. A successful result occurs when the combination of colour, texture, size and shape is balanced.

Choosing Mount Sizes

◀▲ The frames left and above demonstrate how the same image can look completely different when treated in two different ways. A very small image may look lost on a wall if it is displayed individually in a small frame. The large frame pictured on the left has a large expanse of mount (mat) board. It draws the eye into the image in the centre of the frame. This image demands to be looked at. The style shown above would work well as part of a group of similar frames.

◀ Mount pairs or groups of small images together in one frame to increase the picture area. Choose the shape of the picture to suit the position where it will hang. Long rectangular pictures, for instance, can be used to fill the wall space between two windows or doors.

Two methods of securing the artwork to the backing board are shown here. Book mounts are for squared-up images where the picture edges are hidden. A float mount is for images whose edges are on display.

Securing the Artwork

Book mount Paper tapes at the upper edge of the artwork hold it in place, while the mount (mat) and backing board are simply hinged together at the top.

you will need

pre-cut window mount (mat)

artwork

backing board

acid-free hinging tape

self-adhesive fabric tape

1 Make the window at least 5mm/¼in smaller than the image.

2 Stick two short pieces of acid-free tape to the underside of the image.

3 Stick a second piece across the free end of each length of tape to make two tab hinges. There should be a gap between the top of the picture and the second pieces of tape. Leave the tape to dry.

4 Stick a length of self-adhesive fabric tape along the top edge of the backing board so that half of the tape is above the edge. Fold the tape back on itself and crease with the edge of your thumbnail. Position the mount on top and press in place.

Float mount

you will need

pre-cut window mount (mat) (reserving
cut-out section of board)
backing board
artwork
acid-free hinging tape
craft knife
ruler
self-healing cutting mat
self-adhesive fabric tape

This invisible method of mounting is for artwork that is smaller than the aperture. Images printed on handmade paper that has an attractive deckle edge are often mounted in this way.

1 Place the mount (mat) on top of the backing board and position the artwork face down in the window. Tear two 5cm/2in strips of hinging tape, dampen the last 5mm/¼in of each and stick to the artwork approximately 2.5cm/1in from the top.

2 Mark the positions of the paper hinges on the backing board. Using a craft knife and working on a cutting mat, cut two 5mm/¼in slots through the backing board at the marked positions. Cut the slots wide enough to feed the hinges through.

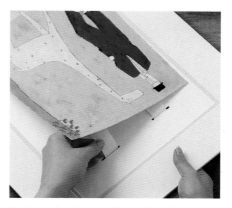

3 Attach the backing board to the window mount as for the book mount opposite. Place the artwork in position and feed the tapes through the slots. Make sure the artwork is in exactly the right position in the mount. Fit the cut-out section from the mount back in the aperture to hold the artwork in position and turn the mount over. Dampen the free ends of the pieces of tape and stick them to the back of the backing board to secure the artwork.

Mouldings are the decoratively shaped lengths of wood used to make up the frame. They are available in a variety of finishes and are always described by their profile – that is, their cross-sections or end-views.

Mouldings

Mouldings are usually sold in 1.8m/6ft or 2.4m/8ft lengths and are available from builders' merchants, timber yards, art suppliers or framers.

There are two basic types of moulding: picture frame moulding and builders' moulding. The main difference between the two is that picture frame moulding includes a pre-cut rebate, a step that accommodates the artwork, mount (mat), glass and backing board and stops them collapsing through the front of the frame.

Builders' moulding is fundamentally intended for trimming internal structures such as door frames, windows and skirting boards, and consequently does not need to incorporate a rebate. To convert builders' moulding it is necessary to create a suitable recess by attaching narrow strips of wood, called fillets, under the moulding before assembling the frame.

Manufactured moulding is often pre-decorated and finished. Many styles are available, from reproduction, antiqued, metal and highly decorated, to plain wood. Natural wood mouldings leave the embellishment in the hands of the framer. Ash and oak have a pleasing grain, and lime-waxing or woodstaining enhances it. Obeche and ramin are woods that are suitable for more opaque or solid decoration. One factor to take into consideration is whether the wood is a softwood or a hardwood. For example, ash and oak are very hard and take some perseverance to cut, whereas obeche, pine and ramin are fairly easy to cut.

▼

Multiple lengths of moulding make a dramatic deep frame for a tiny image.

▼

This modern gilded frame sets off the golden leaves in the picture.

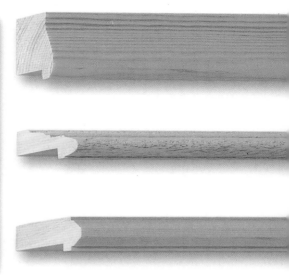

▲

Use a subtle bamboo-effect moulding, to enhance an image with an Oriental theme. The width of the frame also mirrors the width of the leaves and adds a delicacy to this large picture.

▲

A small but powerful image stands out well in an opulent frame.

▶

A slim moulding looks elegant around a small image in a large mount (mat).

▼

This colourwashed moulding has a ripple effect that echoes the waves on the sea. Its rough wood finish looks a little like driftwood and the bold colour suits the naive image perfectly.

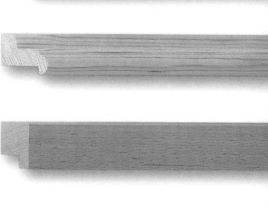

There are several ways of cutting a length of moulding to make a basic frame, but the ends must always be cut at a precise angle. You can use either a mitre clamp or a wooden mitre box to guide the saw.

Cutting and Joining a Basic Frame

you will need

tape measure

moulding

mitre clamp or box

saw

pencil

PVA (white) glue and brush

frame clamp

cloth

V-nail joiner and V-nails or vice,

panel pins (brads) and tack hammer

woodfiller

cork sanding block

medium- and fine-grade sandpaper

(glasspaper)

1 Measure the mounted artwork to give you the inside rebate measurement for the frame. Hold the length of moulding in a mitre clamp or box and cut the first end at a 45° angle. The edge of the moulding with the rebate should be the furthest from you.

2 Measure along the inside rebate of the moulding and mark the position for the next mitre cut on the face of the moulding.

3 Insert the moulding in the mitre clamp or box and saw at a 45° angle along the marked line.

4 Place the moulding in the mitre clamp or box. To make the next section of the frame, cut away the triangular "offcut" as in step 1 with the same 45° angle. Do this before you measure the second cut.

5 Measure and mark the second cut on the moulding. Repeat the steps until all four lengths are cut. Check that each pair – the two side lengths and the lengths for the top and bottom – is an exact match.

6 Using PVA (white) glue, secure two sections of the moulding together to make a right angle. Repeat with the other sections, then join them all together to make the frame.

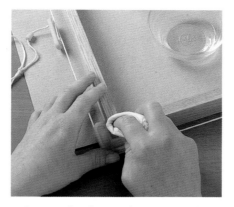

7 Secure the frame clamp around the frame to hold the glued pieces together. Wipe away any excess glue with a damp cloth before it begins to set, otherwise it will form a waterproof barrier sealing the wood and any colourwash or woodstain you choose to use will not stain the wood around the joints.

8 Turn the frame right side down and insert V-nails into the corners of the back of the frame using a hand-held underpinner tool. Or, place the right-angled corners of the frame in a vice, and hammer panel pins (brads) into the corner edges of the moulding using a tack hammer. Once all four corners have been pinned, leave to dry.

9 Turn the frame right side up and fill the mitred corners with woodfiller. Wipe away any excess woodfiller with a damp cloth. Allow to dry.

10 Use a cork block and medium-grade sandpaper (glasspaper) to sand all over the frame and the rebate. Repeat with finer-grade sandpaper.

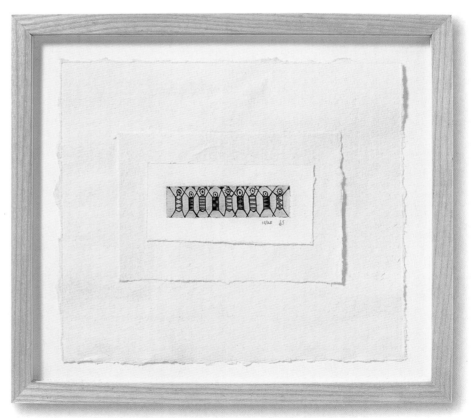

Builder's architrave, used for skirting boards and door frames, can be used to make sturdy inexpensive frames. Architrave is flat on the reverse, so to enable it to hold a picture, glass and backing board you need to create a rebate.

Creating a Rebate

Using a router

you will need

power router

rebate cutter with ball-bearing pilot tip

spanner

2 G-clamps

2 lengths of architrave

A power router is quick to set up and the finished results are very profes-sional. Edge-forming cutters have a rotating tip that runs along the edge of the wood. The rebate can be cut on lengths of moulding before making up the frame, or on the finished frame.

1 Select a rebate cutter with a ball-bearing pilot tip. An edge-forming pilot tip allows the router to run along the edge of the architrave without a guide rail. Ensure the router is switched off, loosen the collet nut and fit the rebate cutter. Tighten the collet nut with a spanner.

2 Clamp the length of architrave face down on a workbench. Clamp a sec-ond length in front of it on which to balance the router. Adjust the depth scale on the side of the router to the exact depth of the rebate required.

◄ **3** Balance the router on the two pieces of wood. Switch it on and use the plunge mechanism to drop the router on to the depth stop. Tighten the plunge-lock handle. Holding the router with both hands, advance the router into the architrave, using light pressure to move it along the length of the wood. Release the plunging mech-anism when you reach the end and switch off.

Using fillets

you will need

tape measure

builder's architrave

mitre box or clamp

saw

wood glue and brush

frame clamp

V-nails

V-nail joiner

mallet (optional)

fillet of wood

hammer

panel pins (brads)

Create a rebate by fitting lengths of wood, called fillets, on the reverse side of the frame. The depth of the wood should be the same as the required rebate – usually 1cm/½in. The width of the wood must be at least 5mm/¼in narrower than the architrave, but if you do not want to see the fillet at the outer edge of the frame the width should be narrower still.

1 Measure the artwork to determine the inside measurement of the frame. Cut the first end of the architrave with a mitre saw set at 45°. Measure the length required on the inside edge of the architrave. Turn the saw to the other side and line it up against the mark. Cut the second end. Cut two pieces of architrave for the sides and two for the top and bottom of the frame. Spread the cut ends with glue and assemble the frame.

2 Fit a frame clamp on each corner and tighten the cord. Leave the glue to dry thoroughly.

3 Turn the frame over. Put a V-nail on the magnetic tip of the V-nail joiner with the sharp edge up. Check that the V-nail is correctly positioned across the joint and push down firmly. Repeat at each corner of the frame. You may need to use a mallet to drive the nails into harder woods.

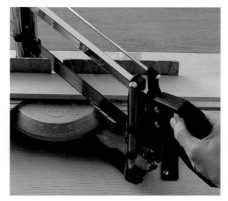

4 Cut the fillet at 45° at one end. Add 1cm/½in to the inside length measurement of the frame, to allow for the rebate, and mark the fillet. Turn the saw to the other side. Line it up with the mark and cut the other end. Cut four pieces of fillet – one for each side of the frame.

5 Spread glue on the underside of the fillet pieces and arrange on the reverse side of the architrave frame. Butt the mitred corners together so that the rebate is the same depth all the way around. Hammer a panel pin (brad) through the fillet and into the architrave every 5cm/2in along each length and leave to dry.

Combine two or three picture-framing mouldings to make your own made-to-measure frame. Two treatments are given to the mouldings chosen for this project: black stain, and a natural polyurethane varnish.

Using Decorative Mouldings

Black Frame

1 Using a tenon saw, cut 20cm/8in lengths from each piece of moulding. Using wood glue, join a barley twist and a semi-circular moulding strip to each side of the flat moulding. (The semicircular moulding will form the rebate of the frame.) Allow the glue to dry completely.

2 Mitre the lengths of assembled moulding using a mitre block and tenon saw, and make up the frame (see Pressed Flowerhead Frame steps 1–4). Mitre the remaining barley twist moulding and glue around the centre front of the frame. Allow to dry.

3 Stain the frame with black ink or woodstain applied with a paintbrush.

4 When the stain is dry, seal the wood and add a sheen with black shoe polish, applied with a soft cloth. Buff it up with a shoe brush.

Natural Frame

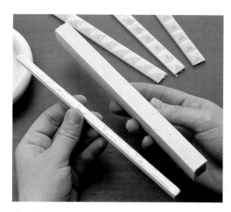

1 Using a tenon saw, cut four 20cm/8in lengths of square moulding. Cut four pieces of flat moulding to the same length. Glue a piece of square moulding to one edge of each piece of flat moulding.

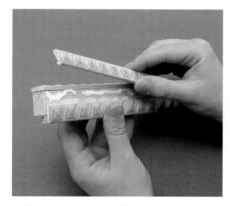

2 Cut 12 pieces of decorative moulding, each 20cm/8in long. Glue two decorative mouldings to the front surface and one on the side. Leave the glue to dry thoroughly.

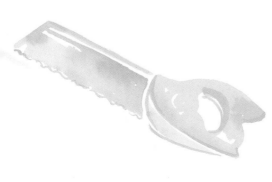

3 Mitre the ends of the assembled pieces, using a mitre block and tenon saw. Glue and clamp the corners accurately together.

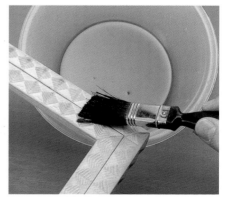

4 Apply one or more coats of clear polyurethane varnish to seal the wood and enhance the natural colours and grain of the wood.

You can use a mitre saw to make frames with more than four corners. To make a hexagonal frame the moulding is cut at an angle of 60°. The blade angle is usually indicated on the clamp, making the cutting process foolproof.

Hexagonal Frame

1 Clamp the mitre saw to the work surface so that you get a smooth cutting action. Move the blade to the 60° mark on the mitre saw. Place the moulding under the saw so that the end juts out beyond the blade. Clamp it in place and cut the first angle.

2 Loosen the clamp and move the moulding along to the required length. Mark the length with a pencil or use the ruler on the mitre clamp. Turn the saw to 60° on the opposite side and cut the moulding.

3 Turn the saw back to the other side. Move the moulding along so that it juts out beyond the blade again ready to cut the second piece. Repeat the steps above to cut six identical pieces.

4 Trim the saw whiskers from the back of each piece of moulding with a craft knife. Spread a little wood glue on both ends of each piece. Arrange and join the pieces on a flat surface and clamp with a frame clamp. Leave the glue to dry overnight.

5 Turn the frame over to the reverse side. Push two V-nails into each joint with a V-nail joiner. If the wood is too hard, tap the end of the tool with a hammer. Remove the frame clamp and polish the frame with wax.

Right: For an octagonal frame set the angle of the mitre saw to 45 degrees.

Instead of making a mitre at each corner, this design for a sturdy frame employs halving joints, cut using a saw and chisel. Halving joints rely on glue for their strength but can be reinforced with dowels or screws.

Halving Joint Frame

you will need

tape measure

pencil

12 x 50mm/½ x 2in wood

tenon saw

T-square

bench hook

clamp

chisel and mallet

wood glue and glue brush

5mm/¼in dowel

drill and 5mm/¼in drill bit

tack hammer

medium- and fine-grade sandpaper

(glasspaper)

1 Measure the artwork horizontally and vertically to determine the aperture size of the frame. Add twice the width of the wood to each measurement to find the length and width of the frame. Cut two pieces of wood the length and two the width of the frame.

2 Use one of the cut pieces to mark the width of the wood at both ends of each piece. Use the square to mark the wood across the width and down the side. Mark the centre line on both sides at each end of the wood.

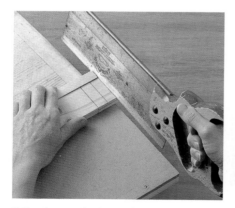

3 Fit the marked wood against a bench hook and saw along the line through to the halfway mark, bringing the saw to the horizontal to make a straight cut. Make two or three further saw cuts to make chiselling out the waste easier.

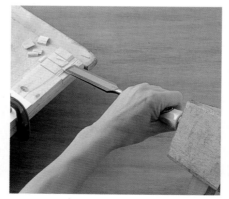

4 Secure the wood to the bench with a clamp. Using the chisel and a mallet cut away the waste wood above the line. Turn the wood round and chisel out from the other side.

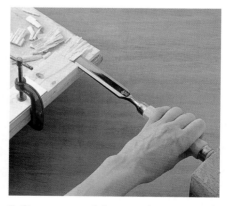

5 Once most of the wood is removed, work with the chisel horizontally to remove the remaining raised portion in the middle. Cut all four frame pieces in the same way with the cut joints on the same side.

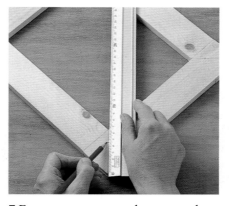

6 Turn the side sections over to the reverse side and assemble the frame. Glue the cut surfaces of the joints and clamp together. Check the corners are square and leave to dry.

7 For a stronger, more decorative dowelled joint, mark a diagonal line from the corner of the aperture to the outer corner of the frame. Measure along this line to mark the dowel positions. Cut eight pieces of dowel the same depth as the frame.

8 Clamp the frame to scrap wood and drill through at each mark. Drop a little glue into each hole. Tap the pieces of dowel into the holes and leave to dry. Sand the edges of the joints so that they are flush with the frame.

you will need

wooden frame

4 decorative frame corners

PVA (white) glue and brush

acrylic paint

paintbrush

varnish or wax

Adding decorative corners

To give a plain frame a more individual appearance, add decorative corners and paint them to match the frame. Corners are available in a variety of styles and sizes and are sold by most art and picture framing suppliers.

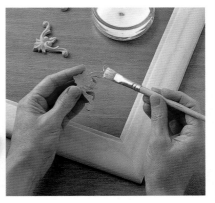

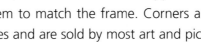

1 Apply glue to the reverse of each frame corner in turn, then position them at each corner of the frame. Leave to dry on a flat surface.

2 Cover the frame, including the corners, with two coats of acrylic paint and leave to dry. Varnish or wax the frame as required.

The traditional cross-over frame, often known as a school frame, is quite easy to make. The skill is in making each joint exactly the right size so that the sides of the frame fit securely together.

Cross-over Frame

you will need

tape measure

length of square section wood,
15mm/⅝in wide

pencil

tenon saw

bench hook or vice

G-clamp

chisel

flat surform file

coarse sandpaper (glasspaper)

fine sanding pad

PVA (white) glue and brush

board and weight

rubber (latex) gloves

soft cloths

dark woodstain

black patinating wax

1 Measure the artwork and mount (mat) board horizontally and vertically to find the aperture size of the frame. Add 9cm/3½in to each measurement to determine the lengths of wood required for the frame. Cut two lengths and two widths.

2 Mark the wood 9cm/3½in from each end. Use a spare piece of the wood to mark the width of the joint and square the lines. Mark the halfway line on each side of the wood. Fit the wood in a bench hook or vice. Saw just inside each line down to the halfway mark. Turn the wood around and cut the other end in the same way. Cut all four pieces.

3 Clamp the wood to the bench and chisel out the waste wood a little at a time. On narrow wood strips use the chisel vertically with the flat surface towards the marked line. Push down firmly to remove the wood bit by bit.

4 To shape the edges of the frame, hold a flat surform file at an angle across the edge of the wood. File the wood between the chiselled-out sections until there is a 3–5mm/⅛–¼in flat surface that tapers off at each end.

5 Shape the ends of each piece using the surform. This time the shaped edge is tapered near the cut-out section and then comes right off the end rather than tapering again. Shape the ends of each piece.

6 Sand all the shaped edges with coarse sandpaper (glasspaper) until they are smooth and rounded. Finish off with a fine sanding pad.

7 To assemble the frame, arrange the top and bottom sections of the frame the correct distance apart. Spread glue on all the sides of the cut-out sections of one of the side pieces and fit in place. Glue the other side in place. Place a board and weight on top of the frame until the glue dries.

8 Using a soft cloth, wipe the wood with a dark woodstain, making sure there is no bare wood showing in any inside corners around the cross-over joints. Leave to dry. To finish the frame, rub black patinating wax into the wood and buff up the surface with a clean cloth.

Any shape of frame can be cut from medium density fibreboard using a carpenter's jigsaw. Draw your design and simply cut around it. You can cut the rebate into the aperture using a router.

Jigsaw Puzzle Frame

you will need

pencil

cardboard

craft knife

cutting mat

medium-density fibreboard (MDF),
9mm/⅜in thick

marker pen

2 G-clamps

protective face mask

jigsaw with 2mm/¹⁄₁₆in blade suitable
for MDF

ruler

piece of scrap wood

drill and 8mm/⁵⁄₁₆in bit

medium-grade sandpaper (glasspaper)

fine sanding pad

router with rebate cutter

cloth

acrylic paint

paintbrush

backing board

panel pins (brads)

tack hammer

1 Draw a jigsaw puzzle shape template on cardboard and cut it out using a craft knife and working on a cutting mat. Place the template on the medium density fibreboard (MDF) and draw around it using a marker pen. Clamp the MDF to the workbench so that the line you are going to cut first is clear of the bench. Wear a protective face mask when working with MDF to avoid inhaling dust particles.

2 Using a jigsaw, cut one side of the frame just outside the drawn line. Turn the template around to the next side. Continue turning and cutting until all four sides are cut.

3 In each corner of the aperture, draw an 8mm/⁵⁄₁₆in square using a pencil and ruler and mark across each square on the diagonal to find its centre.

4 Place the frame on a piece of scrap wood and clamp in position. Drill through the MDF into the scrap wood at each centre point. Secure the frame to the workbench so that the first side of the aperture is clear of the work surface. Cut along the line between the two holes. Turn the frame around and cut the other sides in turn.

5 Sand the frame edges. If you are making frames to link together, check the fit. Adjust as necessary. Finish the frame with a fine sanding pad.

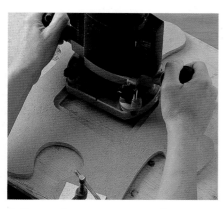

6 Fit a rebate cutter into the router. Clamp the frame face down on the workbench. Set the router depth. Place the router in the aperture. Cut out the rebate, then sand the frame. Wipe the surface with a damp cloth.

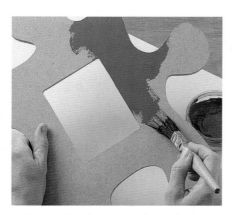

7 Paint the frame as desired. Cut a backing board to fit the aperture. Insert the picture, then the backing, and secure with panel pins (brads).

Similar in effect to a multi-window mount (mat), this frame is ideal for collections of objects – in this case, pressed leaves – and creates a dramatic three-dimensional effect. Finish the surface with Danish oil.

Multi-window Frame

you will need

tape measure

T-square

pencil

18mm/¾in birch plywood:

2 front verticals, 60 x 6cm/

24 x 2½in; 4 front horizontals,

13 x 7cm/5 x 2¾in;

back, 60 x 25cm/24 x 10in

jigsaw

tenon saw

medium- and fine-grade sandpaper

(glasspaper)

cork sanding block

PVA (white) glue and glue brush

self-adhesive sealing tape

scissors

soft cloths

Danish wood oil

dish

rubber (latex) gloves

sheer fabric

metal ruler

craft knife

heavy weights or G-clamps

tack hammer

large-headed nails, 2.5cm/1in long

epoxy resin glue and brush

pressed leaves

1 With a tape measure, T-square and pencil, mark the lengths and widths of the plywood and saw the pieces to size. Butt the plywood pieces together to check that they fit. Cut the back of the frame and set aside. Sand down all the edges.

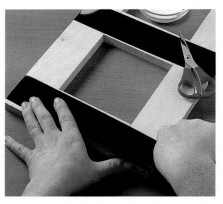

2 Apply PVA (white) glue to the ends of the horizontals and assemble the frame. Wrap self-adhesive sealing tape around the frame, both front and back. Wipe off the excess glue at once with a damp cloth and leave overnight to dry.

3 Once the glue has set, remove the tape. Use medium-grade sandpaper (glasspaper) with a cork sanding block to sand the face and all edges of the frame. For a smooth finish, sand again with fine-grade sandpaper.

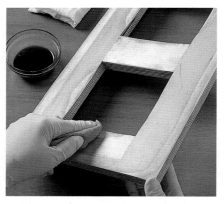

4 Place some Danish wood oil in a dish. Wearing rubber (latex) gloves, apply the oil over the wood in a circular motion using a soft cloth. Work the oil into the wood. Buff up with a clean soft cloth.

5 Apply a line of glue to the front of the backing board, approximately 3cm/1¼in in from the edge. Stick the fabric on to it. Leave to dry.

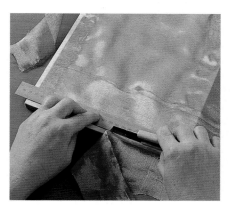

6 Trim the excess fabric using a metal ruler and craft knife.

7 Apply glue to the back of the frame front, then align the frame front and backing board and stick the two halves together.

8 Place heavy weights or G-clamps on each corner and the middle section of the frame. Place a cloth below the weights or clamps to prevent damage to the face of the frame. Wipe away excess glue with a damp cloth and leave to dry overnight.

9 Apply a coat of oil to the side edges of the backing board. Find the centre of each window and hammer in a large-headed nail, leaving approximately 1cm/½in showing. Mix a small amount of epoxy resin glue and apply this to the nail heads. Place a leaf on each nail and leave to set.

Good, clean driftwood can be hard to find even if you live near the sea, but you can make your own "driftwood" from old boards or packing crates. Break up the wood and distress the lengths with a chisel.

Driftwood Frame

you will need

packing crate or wooden board

chisel

hammer

surform file

coarse-grade sandpaper (glasspaper)

watercolour paints: green, crimson and blue

paintbrushes

epoxy resin glue

coping saw

hardboard

chalkboard paint

masking tape

drill

sisal string, 1m/1⅛ yd

scissors

thick sisal rope, 1m/1⅛ yd

1 Split the wood into narrower lengths using a chisel and a hammer.

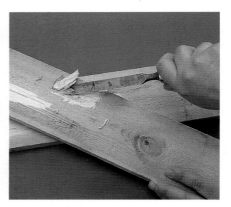

2 Select four suitable lengths of similar width for the sides of the frame. Gouge chunks from the sides of the wood to make it look weatherbeaten.

4 Sand the wood down with coarse-grade sandpaper (glasspaper) to remove any splinters, and round off the edges.

5 Mix a thin colourwash using green, crimson and blue watercolour paints and brush it on to the wood. Allow the wood to dry.

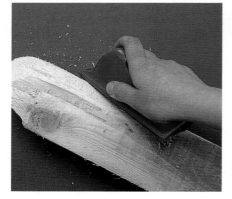

3 Use a surform to file away the edges of the wood until they are smooth.

6 Glue the frame together with epoxy resin glue and allow to dry. Cut a piece of hardboard to fit the back of the frame and paint the smooth side with chalkboard paint.

7 Tape the chalkboard to the back of the frame. Drill a hole in each corner through all the layers. Thread each end of a length of sisal string through the holes at the bottom of the frame, working from the back to the front. Knot the ends on the front of the frame. Trim any excess string.

8 Enlarge the two holes at the top of the frame and pass thick sisal rope through the holes as before, leaving enough excess rope to hang the frame. Tie a knot in each end on the front of the frame.

Reclaimed timber has a natural distressed and heavy appearance. This frame requires no finish, relying instead on its natural characteristics for its rugged appeal.

Reclaimed Timber Frame

you will need

reclaimed timber:

2 verticals, 62 x 10cm/25 x 4in

2 horizontals, 18 x 10cm/7 x 4in

tape measure

pencil

tenon saw

sandpaper (glasspaper)

hardboard, 54 x 28cm/22 x 11in

coping saw

fabric glue and brush

black felt

decorative paper

PVA (white) glue and brush

chalk

bradawl (awl)

14 screws, 2.5cm/1in long

screwdriver

4 reclaimed brackets

8 galvanized nails, 2.5cm/1in long

hammer

fillets, 5mm/¼in deep

natural objects for framing

1 On the timber, measure and mark with a pencil the length and width of the frame verticals and horizontals. Use a tenon saw to cut the timber to the correct sizes. Lightly sand the sawn edges. Cut the hardboard backing board to size. Apply fabric glue to the back, then stick a piece of black felt on top. Glue decorative paper to the face of the backing board.

2 Mark out corner holes for the screws, using chalk. Turn the cut lengths of timber face down and butt them together at the corners. Place the felt-covered hardboard on the back of the timber. Make initial holes in the hardboard with a bradawl (awl), then screw into the back of the frame. The screws will hold the frame together.

3 Turn the frame the right way up and nail in the reclaimed brackets, using galvanized nails.

4 Cut small fillets to size, coat with PVA (white) glue, and use them to mount the framed objects to give a three-dimensional effect.

A deep-sided, sectioned frame is the perfect way to display a collection of small objects such as ornaments, jewellery or badges. Custom-build the sections to suit the size of the objects in your collection.

Box Frame

you will need

length of batten, 30 x 5mm/1¼ x ¼ in

pencil

metal ruler

junior hacksaw

wood glue

panel pins (brads)

hammer

hardboard

jigsaw or coping saw

white acrylic primer

paintbrush

length of batten, 30 x 2mm/1¼ x 1⁄16 in

masking tape

PVA (white) glue and brush

tissue paper in assorted colours

acrylic paint: yellow and blue

artist's brushes

small Indian shisha glass

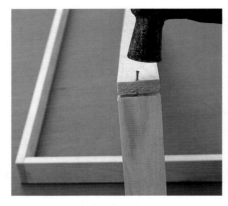

1 Using the thicker battening, measure and cut four sides of the rectangular frame, then glue them together with wood glue and secure with panel pins (brads).

2 Cut a piece of hardboard to fit the frame and paint the smooth front side with acrylic primer. When dry, glue and pin it to the back of the frame.

4 Assemble the compartments inside the box frame with wood glue, taping them in position with masking tape until the glue has set.

5 Coat the inside of each compartment with PVA (white) glue and cover with pieces of torn tissue paper. Work the tissue paper into the corners and keep applying the glue. Use light colours over strong colours to create depth.

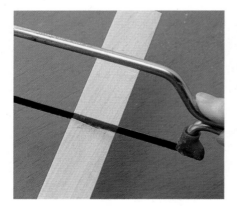

3 Measure and draw out all the compartments. Cut the dividers from the length of thinner battening.

6 Carefully retouch any areas of the compartments that need more colour, using yellow acrylic paint. Allow the paint to dry.

7 Use wood glue to attach lengths of the thinner battening to the outer edge of the frame, in effect creating a rebate. Leave the glue to dry.

8 Cover the edge of the frame with a collage of blue tissue paper, using PVA glue.

9 Using an artist's brush, lightly brush over the tissue paper with blue acrylic paint. Leave to dry.

10 Glue small Indian shisha glass all around the frame. Arrange your collection in the compartments, securing the pieces with glue.

In this type of frame, the artwork sits flush with the face of the frame. A gap is left around the edge of the canvas to give it depth. Here the frame is colourwashed to match the colours in the painting.

Framing a Canvas

you will need

tape measure

painted, stretched canvas

pencil

wooden frame, prepared and sanded

gouache paint: ultramarine and black

paintbrush

bowl

cloth

batten, 2.5cm/1in wide, 5mm/¼in deep

tenon saw

hardboard

jigsaw or coping saw

emulsion (latex) paint: black

PVA (white) glue and brush

framer's point gun

panel pins (brads) and tack hammer (optional)

bradawl (awl)

screws, 1cm/½in long

screwdriver

self-adhesive backing tape

craft knife

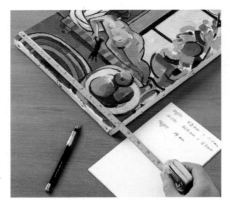

1 Measure the canvas and add on 1cm/½in to the vertical and horizontal measurements. This will give a 5mm/¼in gap around the canvas when it is eventually inserted into the frame. Measure the depth of the canvas and choose a frame that is deep enough to allow the canvas to lie flush with the face of the frame.

2 Mix two parts ultramarine gouache with one part black gouache in a bowl. Blend together and add four parts water. Mix well with a paintbrush. This is a very opaque colourwash solution. Apply the wash in long, smooth strokes on the face and then the side edges of the frame. Leave to dry.

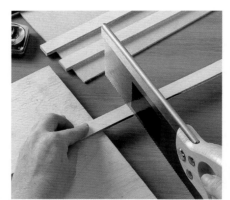

3 Place the frame face down on a piece of cloth. Measure the inside vertical and horizontal edges of the frame. These measurements are for the fillets and the backing board. Mark and saw the fillets and the hardboard to fit inside the rebate.

4 Using black emulsion (latex) paint, paint one face and edge of all the fillets and a strip approximately 5cm/2in wide around the edge of the face of the hardboard. Leave to dry. Neatly paint the edge of the canvas.

5 Once the fillets have dried, apply PVA (white) glue to the unpainted side of each one and place them around the sides of the frame.

6 When the fillets are secure, place the backing board, painted side facing inwards, in the frame and pin in position, using a framer's point gun. Alternatively use panel pins (brads) and a tack hammer.

7 Place the canvas in the frame and hold it in place. On the back make a hole aligning with each corner of the canvas using a bradawl (awl). Screw the hardboard to the canvas. Tape up the back of the frame.

If the image you are going to frame is simple and plain, you can add decorative interest by insetting objects into the frame. Choose a wide moulding with enough depth to allow shapes to be chiselled out.

Insetting Objects into a Frame

1 Mark out oblongs and squares on the face of the frame with a ruler and soft pencil. Centre the shapes between the rebate and outside edge.

2 Score the pencil marks on the frame using a craft knife and a metal ruler. Chisel out the shapes quite deeply, so that the glass will not protrude from the face of the frame.

3 Sand the frame with medium-grade sandpaper (glasspaper) and a cork sanding block, then with a finer grade of sandpaper.

4 Using a soft cloth and wearing rubber (latex) gloves, apply olive green oil paint over the frame. Cut pieces of black cardboard for the background of each inset, and glue in place in the chiselled-out spaces.

5 Cut the glass for all the inserts to the sizes required using a glass cutter and a T-square. Decorate the underside of some pieces of the insert glass with Dutch metal leaf for an opaque effect. Spray a few of the glass pieces with a little glass etching spray, ensuring that the objects underneath will remain visible. Wear a protective face mask and work in a ventilated area.

6 Select the objects to be inserted in the inset panels. To decorate the glass for the slate pebbles, place masking tape in two strips over the glass and spray on the etching spray in a line down the centre, holding the can about 20cm/8in away. When the spray is dry, remove the tape to reveal a neat line of mottled glass.

7 Mark and cut out cardboard fillets to the appropriate size. Glue the fillets into the chiselled oblongs.

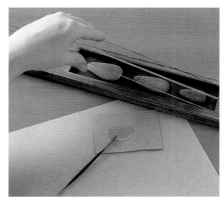

8 Glue the slate pebbles on to the black cardboard background using epoxy resin. Glue the glass on to the fillets using epoxy resin.

9 Add other decorative elements to the frame as desired. If the objects are flat, attach them to the glass with PVA glue, which will dry transparent.

Birch plywood is used in this unusual frame because of its strength. The heavier the stone you wish to frame, the thicker the plywood needs to be. For a heavy stone, replace the galvanized nails with strong screws.

Framing an Engraved Stone

you will need

tape measure

birch plywood, 18mm/¾in thick

tenon saw

drill and masonry bit

medium- and fine-grade sandpaper (glasspaper)

cork sanding block

rubber (latex) gloves

oil paint: olive green

soft cloths

galvanized nails, 2.5cm/1in long

tack hammer

1 Measure and saw the birch plywood to fit the stone plaque, allowing for a border of approximately 4cm/1½in all round. Using a drill with a masonry bit, drill four holes in the stone, one in each of the corners.

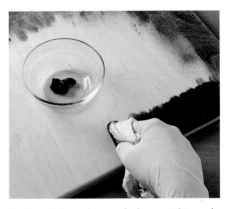

2 Sand the plywood, first with medium-, then fine-grade sandpaper (glasspaper), using a cork sanding block to smooth it down. Wearing rubber (latex) gloves, apply olive green oil paint with a soft cloth all over the plywood. Rub it well into the grain and buff with a clean, soft cloth.

3 Place the stone on the plywood and level up. Place a cloth over the galvanized nails to avoid marking the stone when you hammer them in through the drilled holes.

The decoration on this wide, flat frame uses a wonderfully simple technique to achieve the look of hand lettering. Photocopies of lettering, or even pictures, may be used in the same way.

Decorative Lettering

you will need

wooden frame, prepared and sanded

computer-generated text

scissors

plain paper

masking tape

rubber (latex) gloves

silkscreen cleaner

soft cloths

protective face mask

clear car spray lacquer

1 Choose a moulding with a wide, flat face. Cut the printed text into strips and place it face down on plain paper, securing it with masking tape. Wearing rubber (latex) gloves, pour a small amount of silkscreen cleaner on to a piece of cloth. Gently wipe the cloth over the back of the paper bearing the text. Then, using a dry cloth, wipe over the photocopy again to transfer a reverse image of the text on to the plain paper.

2 Secure the reversed text to the frame text side down, using masking tape. Gently apply silkscreen cleaner to the paper. Using a dry cloth, wipe over the paper. Remove the applied text and leave to dry for 10 minutes.

3 Transfer the text all around the frame. Wearing a protective face mask, apply a coat of car spray lacquer over the frame to seal the lettering.

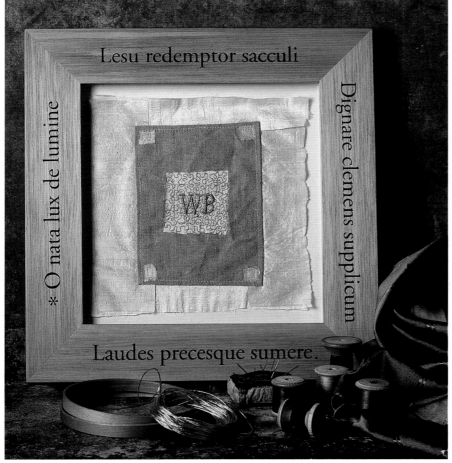

Glass is required on any artwork needing protection from atmospheric pollution and ultraviolet rays, which in time will cause a picture to fade. Different types of glass suit different framing purposes.

Choosing Glass

The type of glass used in picture framing is known as float glass, which is of a higher quality and clarity than sheet glass which is normally used for glazing windows and doors. The most commonly used is 2mm/¹⁄₁₆in thick. For more precious artwork, museum glass is used; although extremely expensive, it is the best protection for artwork and it is almost invisible.

Clear glass

The staple glass for picture framing, clear glass is generally 2mm/¹⁄₁₆in thick, which is the optimum thickness for strength and ease of cutting. This glass has a shiny surface that reflects light and causes a mirror-effect in some situations. For reasons of safety, 2mm/¹⁄₁₆ in glass is used only up to a certain size, approximately 1m/1⅛ yd across. For areas larger than this, heavy-duty glass 4–6mm/⅛–¼in thick should be used.

Non-reflective glass

This has a slightly frosted or cloudy appearance because one side of the glass is etched with hydrochloric acid to create a surface that breaks up the reflected light. As only 87 per cent of transmitted light passes through the glass, the image becomes increasingly diffused if it is mounted in a double or triple mount (mat).

Anti-reflective glass

This glass allows 98 per cent of transmitted light to pass through. It is almost invisible over artwork and as a result is sometimes known as "magic" glass. Its anti-reflective properties are effective from all angles.

Perspex (plexiglass)

Clear acrylic sheet is a lightweight, non-breakable alternative to clear glass. It is ideal for protecting pictures that are to hang in busy public areas, on business premises or in children's rooms where safety is a priority.

Glass suppliers will cut glass to size for you at the time of purchase, but you may also need to cut pieces yourself if you are doing a lot of framing. The skill needs a confident but careful approach.

Cutting Glass

you will need

frame

tape measure

protective cotton gloves

fine black marker pen

picture glass

T-square

glass cutter

piece of board

pencil

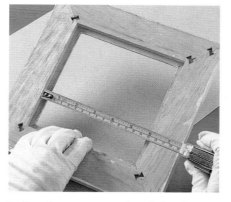

1 On the reverse side of the frame, measure the horizontal from rebate to rebate. Wear protective cotton gloves when you are handling glass.

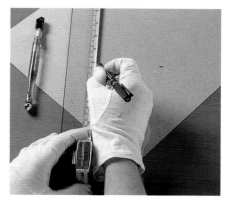

2 Reduce the window measurement by 2mm/¹⁄₁₆in, then mark the measurement on the glass using a fine black marker pen.

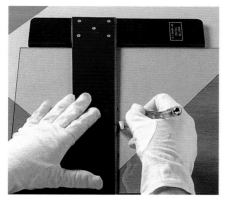

3 Place a T-square on the glass and line up the glass cutter so that it is on top of the marks. Holding both the glass cutter and T-square, firmly score the glass with the glass cutter in one long smooth stroke. Do not cut again over the same line, as this will make the glass shatter and splinter.

4 Hold the glass over a board so that the score line is on the edge. Gently tap the glass below the score mark, using the round end of the cutter.

5 Place a pencil directly beneath the cut. Using both hands placed on each side of the pencil and score mark, gently but firmly press the glass down. The glass will break cleanly along the score line. Repeat for the vertical measurement. When the glass is cut, clean it, then gently insert it in the rebate at the back of the frame.

"Fitting up" is the process of fixing the artwork into the frame itself. It is advisable to follow the simple steps below and assemble the sections in the correct order.

Fitting up a Frame

you will need

tape measure
frame
pencil
picture glass
glass cutter
protective cotton gloves
fine black marker pen
T-square
piece of board
white sheet
methylated spirits (denatured alcohol)
soft cloth
mounted artwork
backing board
framer's points or panel pins (brads)
point gun or hammer
self-adhesive sealing tape
craft knife
bradawl (awl) or drill and bit
2 D-rings
screwdriver
picture hanging wire
wire cutters

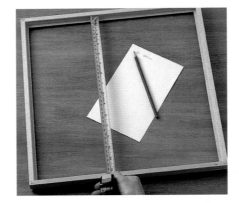

1 Measure the frame inside the rebate horizontally and vertically. Take 2mm/¹⁄₁₆in from each measurement to find the finished glass size. Cut the glass to size.

2 Place the glass on a white sheet so that you can see any blemishes more easily. Clean both sides of the glass with methylated spirits (denatured alcohol) and buff with a soft cloth.

3 Place the mounted artwork on top of the backing board and place the glass on top. Lower the frame on to the glass. Pick up the assembled frame and check that there are no flecks of dust under the glass.

4 Turn the entire frame over and place face down on a folded sheet. Insert framer's points or panel pins (brads) on each side of the frame using a point gun or a hammer. Insert pins near each corner and then one or two in between, approximately 8–10cm/3–4in apart.

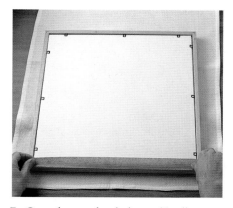

5 Cut the end of the self-adhesive sealing tape straight. Stick the first length down along the first side so that it is approximately 3mm/⅛in away from the edge. Using a craft knife, cut the tape at the other end parallel to the edge of the frame.

6 Turn the frame around. Lay the next length of tape exactly overlapping the end of the first strip and stick along the next edge. Cut the tape off at the end 3mm/⅛in away from the outside edge of the frame. Repeat on the remaining two sides.

7 From the top edge of the picture, measure one-third of the way down each side and mark with a pencil. Use a bradawl (awl) to make a hole or drill a small guide hole at each mark.

8 Choose the size of D-ring fastening to fit within the width of the moulding. Screw a D-ring into the frame at each guide hole.

9 Wrap picture hanging wire twice around the first D-ring and then twist the end around the hanging wire six or seven times so that the coils are tightly packed. The hanging wire should be long enough to go round two widely spaced hooks positioned just below the top of the picture.

10 Tie off the wire around the second D-ring in the same way and cut off the excess wire. Hang the picture from two widely spaced hooks. The wire should rise almost vertically from the D-rings to put the least amount of strain on the frame.

Fillets can be used in picture framing to create a space between the glass and a three-dimensional artwork. Plain wood strips can be used, but the fillets will be visible and should match the frame or the artwork.

Adding Fillets

you will need
tape measure
frame
narrow batten
pencil
cutting mat
craft knife
picture glass
PVA (white) glue and brush

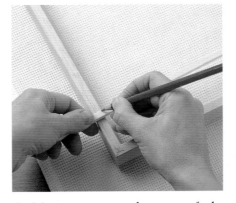

1 Measure across the top of the reverse side of the frame from one side of the rebate to the other. Mark this measurement on the length of batten you are using for the fillets.

2 Lay the batten on a cutting mat and cut to size with a sturdy craft knife. Cut a second piece for the bottom of the frame. Fit these two fillets in the frame then mark and cut two side pieces to fit between them.

3 Place the glass in the frame. Spread glue along the top and bottom pieces of fillet and fit into the frame. Spread glue on the side pieces and stick in position. The side pieces should fit snugly with a neat join at each corner. Leave to dry before inserting the artwork and fitting up the frame.

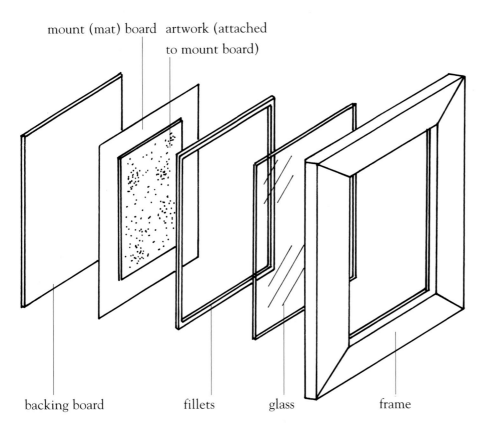

mount (mat) board   artwork (attached to mount board)

backing board   fillets   glass   frame

Picture placement is an art in itself. To conserve your artworks, avoid hanging them near heat sources or in direct sunlight, and never under-estimate the weight of a framed picture.

Hanging Pictures

▲ A muted interior is enhanced by this casually placed picture.

▼ Small pictures make a stronger statement if hung as a group.

▲ Hang pictures at a lower level if you usually view them sitting down.

▼ Framed pictures can be heavy. Invest in proper picture wire cord and fixtures of adequate strength.

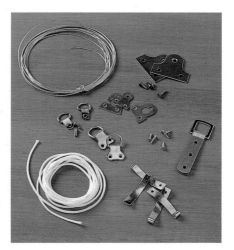

Paint Effects

You can use a wide range of paint effects to brighten and transform existing picture frames. A simple coat of colourwash or woodstain will add instant colour while still allowing the grain of the wood to show through, or you could go for a more dramatic look, such as gilding or a tortoiseshell effect, to create sumptuous style. Add extra decoration with stencils or stamps, and finish with wax or varnish to protect your work.

Playing with Colour

Paint is the most basic material to choose when decorating frames. It comes in any colour you want, it is easy to use, and it creates an immediate impression. However, you don't need to use just paint. You could also try woodstain as an instant dilute covering for wood; ink for penwork decoration; wax, tinted or plain, for a soft sheen; varnish, tinted for an aged look; and glaze to create some of the more complicated effects.

This chapter features a selection of ideas for decorating your frames with paint, glazes and varnish, ranging from the quick and easy to the more sophisticated and time-consuming. So take a look through and have a go at some of the projects. Paint is versatile, and if your first attempt goes wrong, you can simply paint over the top and start again.

Colourwashing and woodstaining are two easy paint effects, both of which use dilute mixes of paint and stain to cover a wooden frame; as the wash and stain are so dilute, the grain of the wood still shows through. You could add further to this

effect, perhaps by gluing extra decoration over the top, or adding penwork or painted motifs. Alternatively you could stencil repeat motifs around the frame, using the colourwash as a background. Other paint techniques include marbling and tor-

toiseshell effects, both of which can be achieved using paint glazes and a little patience. Remember that you are not aiming at an absolute reproduction of marble or tortoiseshell, merely a decorative effect, so don't be nervous about these techniques.

Gilding is another very effective method of transforming a frame. You can cover the frame completely with gold or Dutch metal leaf, or simply apply

squares or cut-out shapes of leaf to the corners or sides of the frame. Then you can distress the gilding for an antiqued effect, or simply seal it to prevent it tarnishing. Paint effects should always be sealed with wax or varnish to protect the surface and make the decoration more durable. Wax provides less protection but gives a softer sheen, whereas varnish is more hardwearing, though not as subtle.

The list below includes the paint and other materials required for the projects in this chapter. Specialist equipment, such as gilder's brushes and metal foils, is available from art and framing suppliers.

Materials and Equipment

Acrylic gesso

Use gesso to provide a smooth base on the surface of the frame before applying painted or gilded decoration. It should be built up in a series of thin coats, and when hard can be sanded to porcelain smoothness or carved and incised in very fine detail.

Agate burnisher

This traditional gilder's tool is used to polish gilding over a gesso surface to a brilliant shine.

Dutch metal leaf

Imitation gold or silver leaf is available either loose or on transfer sheets. It needs to be protected with varnish to prevent tarnishing.

Epoxy glue

This resin glue is a very strong two-part adhesive used to join materials such as metal, stone and glass. Once mixed, it sets in 20 minutes. Mix as much as you need on a piece of scrap card which you can then dispose of.

Epoxy putty

This strong, two-part putty adheres well and can be used to fill small cracks when restoring old frames.

Gelatine capsules

When melted in hot water, these capsules produce an adhering solution for use in the glass-gilding technique known as verre eglomisé.

Gilder's cushion

Used for preparing and cutting loose gold leaf.

Gilder's knife

The knife has a long straight blade for cutting loose gold leaf on a cushion.

Gilder's tip

This wide brush is used for lifting loose leaf on to a sized surface. Wipe it across your face or a smear of petroleum jelly to pick up a little grease before touching it to the leaf.

Gold leaf

Real gold leaf is expensive but produces unrivalled gilding and can be burnished to a bright gleam. It is supplied loose in "books" of 25 sheets.

Liming wax

This consists of clear wax mixed with whiting that collects in wood grain to give a pale limed effect.

Metal polish

This is a fine abrasive cream. It may be used on any surface coated with shellac to give a glossy appearance.

Methylated spirits (denatured alcohol)

This solvent is used as a thinner for woodstain and to clean paintbrushes and glass.

Paint

Gouache is a very opaque, water-based paint that gives a professional finish. **Acrylic** paints are also water-based and are more translucent than gouache. **Oil** paints can be used as a finish, or rubbed into wood grain or a craquelure varnish. **Emulsion (latex)** paint is quick-drying and a good base coat for large projects. **Black patina** is used to give an aged look. **Chalkboard** paint gives a matt black finish.

Paintbrushes

Use sable and flat oil paintbrushes for decoration, household brushes for applying primer and varnishing brushes for protective finishes.

Pigments

These are the purest form of paint and are extremely strong. Use them to tint other media.

Pumice powder

A fine powder abrasive that can be used for distressing gilded surfaces. Different grades are available.

Sandpaper (glasspaper)

Available in different grades, from fine to coarse. Wet-and-dry sandpaper can be rinsed free of dust, making it reusable and longer-lasting. Wrap sandpaper around a cork sanding block when smoothing flat surfaces.

Self-adhesive lead strip

Available in different widths and sold in most hardware stores. It is designed to imitate the lead dividers in stained glass windows.

Shellac

Also known as special pale polish or button polish and used on wood. It is quick-drying and can be tinted to give an antique effect.

Silicone rubber

Cold-curing silicone can be used to make flexible moulds for restoring damaged frame mouldings.

Size

Used in gilding as a mordant. **Oil** size is available with different drying times: the longer the drying time, the shinier the gilding. **Acrylic** size can be used with Dutch metal leaf.

Spray lacquer

Car spray lacquer is available clear or coloured from car maintenance retailers. Work in a well-ventilated area and wear a safety mask.

Stamps

Decorative rubber stamps are available in many designs, or you can make your own from medium density foam.

Stencil card (card stock)

Thin cardboard treated to make it strong and reusable.

Tape

Use masking tape to define areas when painting designs, and to protect mirrors when decorating their frames.

Varnishes

Acrylic varnishes are available in different sheens from high gloss to matt, and have a much faster drying time than spirit (alcohol)-based varnishes. **Craquelure** is a two-part varnish which produces a crackled effect. **Sanding sealer** is quick-drying.

Wax

Clear wax is used to coat and enrich wood. Picture framer's gilt wax is used to disguise repairs to old gilt frames.

White spirit (paint thinner)

This solvent is used for oil size, and for cleaning brushes when using any oil-based products.

Wire (steel) wool

Used for rubbing down and distressing painted or gilded surfaces, and for applying liming wax.

Wood glue

PVA (white) wood glue is used for securing joints in wood.

Woodfiller

Used to fill in gaps on mitred corners and after punching nails into wood. Various types of filler are available.

Woodstain

Available in an abundance of colours and types, from crystals to solutions. Woodstain can be bought from art shops and hardware stores.

Wooden frames are easy to decorate and restore, and can be transformed with many different types of paint finish and decorative paint effects. Gilding is a traditional and beautiful method of decoration.

Paint Techniques

Restoration

Damaged frames need not always be consigned to the rubbish heap. Missing parts of the moulding can be replaced by making plaster casts.

1 Mix some cold-curing silicone, adding curing agent at the ratio of 1 part curing agent to 20 parts silicone base. Mix a small amount of thixotropic additive into the mixture. Once it is the consistency of whipped cream, spread it on to a clean, undamaged section of frame identical to the missing part. Leave to dry for 24 hours, then remove the mould.

2 When the mould is dry, fill it two-thirds full with water then empty the water into a jug. Sprinkle casting plaster into the water until the plaster sits on top and the water no longer absorbs it. Stir thoroughly. Pour the plaster mixture into the mould, and allow to dry for 1 hour. Peel the mould away from the plaster. Trim the cast and fit it in the damaged area of the frame.

Gilding

Traditional gilding techniques using loose gold leaf demand a high degree of skill. Transfer imitation leaf is cheaper and easier to manage.

  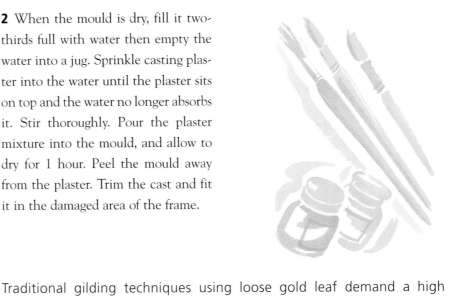

1 Build up a smooth surface for gilding with several coats of gesso or, if using Dutch metal leaf, prepare with red oxide primer. Apply a thin even coat of oil or water-based size to the primed surface, avoiding air bubbles, and leave to become tacky.

2 If you are using loose metal leaf, open the book over a gilder's pad and blow the leaf on to the pad. Ensure the leaf is flat but do not touch it. Brush a gilder's tip over your face or over a smear of petroleum jelly. Touch the tip on the leaf to lift it from the cushion.

3 Use the gilder's tip to touch the leaf to the sized surface, keeping the tip almost parallel with the surface. The leaf will be pulled down by capillary action. Tamp it down gently with cotton wool (cotton balls) to eliminate any air bubbles.

4 If you are using transfer leaf, position the leaf on the sized surface, slightly overlapping the previous one, and rub over the backing paper until the leaf adheres. Lift the paper.

5 Repeat until the whole area is covered. Brush away any loose pieces of leaf with a soft brush: you can save these to be reused later to fill any gaps in the gilding.

6 Seal the surface with wax or polish. Add a few drops of polish to a cloth and apply to the frame. Buff the surface when dry.

Finishing a gilded frame If you feel that a gilded frame is too bright, you can distress or antique the finish, and seal it to prevent it tarnishing. The following techniques are easy ways to achieve a distressed or antiqued look.

Distressing

Antiquing

Sealing

Using fine-grade wire (steel) wool, gently drag it along the leaf in one direction, concentrating on areas that would naturally suffer wear and tear. Moisten a piece of paper towel with white spirit (paint thinner) and gently wipe it over the areas you have distressed, removing the grey particles of wire wool to reveal the undercoat. This can be done as lightly or heavily as you wish. Leave to dry before sealing the surface.

Mix raw umber acrylic paint with a tiny amount of water. Brush it on in one direction, wait a few minutes, then wipe off the surplus with paper towels, wiping in one direction. This leaves a slightly streaky appearance. For a more obviously dragged look, use a slightly dampened flat brush to remove the surplus paint. Allow to dry and then seal.

Use sanding sealer or shellac to seal the leaf and prevent tarnishing. Sanding sealer is virtually colourless, whereas shellac enhances the colour. Brush on an even coat, but try to avoid going over an area twice, or the first layer may start to lift off. Watch for runs and remove them as soon as possible, as both lacquers dry very quickly. Clean the brush immediately in methylated spirits (denatured alcohol). Allow to dry for about an hour.

Paint effects

Many decorative paint effects can be used to rejuvenate old frames. Some, such as tortoiseshell, can look very striking and dramatic, while others, such as colourwashing, have a more subtle effect.

Preparation

Frames should always be prepared before a new paint effect is applied. First, remove the old paint and varnish using a proprietary paint stripper and scraper. It is best to work outdoors or in a well-ventilated room as the fumes can be very strong. Then wash the frame with warm soapy water and a sponge and allow to dry. Finally, rub the frame down with sandpaper (glasspaper) to remove the last traces of old paint and to smooth the surface ready for the new treatment.

Colourwash

Dilute water-based paint and mix thoroughly to make a thin wash. Apply the wash over the frame with a paintbrush, using a single, long, even stroke on each section of the frame. Allow to dry. The wood grain should remain visible beneath the colour.

Liming wax

Liming wax is a mixture of wax and white pigment and can be applied over either a painted or unpainted frame to provide a subtle whitening effect, especially if the wood of the frame is open-grained. Rub the wax into the frame using wire (steel) wool.

Picture framer's gilt wax

This instant finish is useful for covering repairs. Various different shades are available to match existing gilding. You can also use it to add a hint of gold to painted decoration. Apply gilt wax over either a painted or unpainted frame with your finger, then buff with a soft cloth to increase the shine.

Woodstain

Woodstain will colour a wooden frame without concealing the grain of the wood, unlike paint. It is a dilute wash that dries quickly. Apply woodstain with a paintbrush, in even strokes.

Tortoiseshell

This sumptuous paint effect aims to imitate the translucent look of real tortoiseshell. It is achieved by applying diagonal strokes of thin oil glazes in raw umber, burnt sienna and black between many layers of clear shellac varnish. The frame is first gilded to reflect light through the varnish.

Ageing techniques
These techniques create an old, faded look, imitating the effects of time and age on the surface. To look authentic, distressing should concentrate on areas where wear and tear would normally occur.

Distressing

Using fine-grade sandpaper (glass-paper), gently rub down a painted frame to remove some of the paint and reveal the wood beneath. Work carefully, so the distressing is even and not too patchy. Pay particular attention to the corners of the frame.

Using crackle varnish

1 Brush a generous, even coat of the first stage of the crackle varnish over the surface. Check that the surface is completely covered, then leave to dry for 1–3 hours. Test it by lightly touching the varnish with your fingers; it should feel dry but slightly tacky.

3 If no cracks have appeared, speed up the drying process by moving a hairdryer on its coolest setting over the surface, but not too close to the varnish. Stop as soon as cracks appear. If you are unhappy with the finished effect, remove the varnish with a cloth soaked in water and start again.

2 Brush on a layer of the second stage of the varnish, working evenly and in one direction. Leave to dry for 1–2 hours. Hold the frame up to the light to see if any cracks have appeared: the reaction time will depend on the temperature and humidity of the room in which you are working.

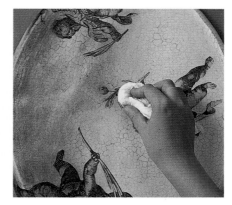

4 Mix raw umber artist's oil paint with a little white spirit (paint thinner). Wipe this mixture in a circular motion all over the surface using paper towels or a soft cloth. Wipe off surplus paint with a clean piece of paper towel, so that the colour is just left in the cracks. Leave to dry thoroughly. Finish with 1–2 layers of oil-based varnish.

Stencils and stamps

Making your own stencils is not difficult, and a lot cheaper than buying ready-cut designs. It is also easy to make your own stamps using high or medium density foam, or even a household sponge.

Transferring a design

1 To transfer a template on to a piece of stencil card (card stock), place a piece of tracing paper over the design, and draw over it with a hard pencil.

2 On the back of the design rub over the lines with a soft pencil. Turn the tracing to the right side and place on top of a sheet of stencil card. Draw over the lines with a hard pencil.

Making a stencil

1 Place the stencil card (card stock) on a cutting mat or piece of thick cardboard and tape in place. Use a craft knife for cutting.

2 It is safer to turn the cutting board as you work so that you are always drawing the knife towards you when cutting around awkward shapes.

Making a stamp

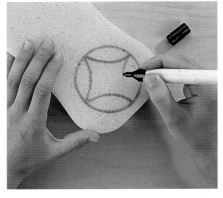

1 Draw a simple design on to a household sponge using a marker pen.

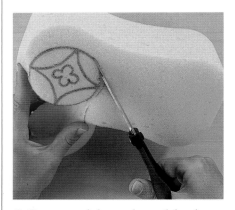

2 Cut around the outline of the design with a pair of sharp scissors. Cut away the unwanted background areas with a craft knife when the outline has been cut. Rinse the completed stamp to remove the remains of the marker ink.

Finishing techniques

Varnish is more hardwearing than wax and gives a matt or glossy finish. Wax offers less protection but it can be replenished from time to time and gives the surface a soft sheen.

Waxing

In addition to providing a protective coating, wax adds a decorative finish. You can use antiquing wax to darken the surface and achieve the look of mahogany or other wood. Apply the wax with a soft cloth and rub it into the wood of the frame, then buff up with a cloth for a soft sheen.

Varnish

Stir the varnish well before using. Coat the brush about halfway up the bristles and lay the varnish on in light strokes, working in one direction. Do not apply too much varnish at a time as this can cause runs. Apply several coats for a protective finish.

Shellac

Shellac can be used to seal bare wood prior to varnishing or painting to prevent the wood from discolouring. It can also be used to seal metal leaf to prevent it tarnishing. Apply shellac with a soft brush or cloth. It will dry very quickly.

Washing brushes

After using paintbrushes, they should always be cleaned straight away. Wash brushes in soapy water if you have been using water-based paint, then rinse in running water, always holding the bristles downwards so they are not damaged by the stream of water. If you have been using oil-based paint or varnish, clean brushes with methylated spirits (denatured alcohol) to remove the paint or varnish.

If your wooden frame has an attractive grain, this simple technique allows you to introduce colour without obscuring the wood's natural qualities. Gouache, acrylic or emulsion (latex) paints are suitable.

Colourwashed Frame

1 Place a walnut-sized amount of violet gouache in a bowl, add a little water and blend in thoroughly. The more water you add, the more translucent the wash will be; if you want a strong colour, add less water. Test the strength of the wash on the back of the frame. When you have the correct dilution, dip a paintbrush into the paint then wipe it against the side of the bowl, removing excess paint.

2 Apply the wash to one section of the face of the frame in one smooth, even stroke, from mitre to mitre. Then paint the side section of the frame. Continue all around the frame. Leave to dry for at least 15 minutes. The more coats of wash applied, the more opaque the colour will appear. Two coats are recommended. Allow to dry.

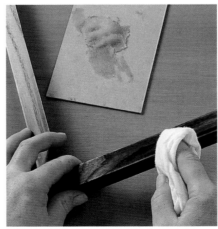

◄ **3** Lightly sand the frame with fine-grade sandpaper (glasspaper) to distress the wash and give a smooth finish. For a wax finish, cover your finger with a cloth, dip it in wax and work it in on a small piece of hardboard to soften the wax. With one long, smooth stroke lightly apply the wax to the frame; do not rub it in as it may remove the wash. Continue all around the frame. Once finished, lightly rub in the wax from where you began. Two or three coats of wax may be necessary.

This project combines all the creative possibilities of stamping. It involves four processes: painting the background, stamping in one colour, over-printing in a second colour and rubbing back.

Stamped Star Frame

you will need

wooden frame, prepared and sanded

emulsion (latex) paint: sky blue, red-brown and gold

paintbrush

palette or plate

foam roller

small and large star stamps

fine wire (steel) wool

1 Paint the frame blue and leave to dry. Put some red-brown paint on a palette and run a foam roller through it until evenly coated. Use the roller to ink a small star stamp and print it in the middle of each side of the frame.

2 Using the red-brown paint, stamp a large star over each corner of the frame. Leave to dry.

3 Ink the large stamp with gold and over-print the corner stars. Allow to dry before rubbing the frame gently with wire (steel) wool.

The stylish raised leaf patterns around this pair of frames are simple to create using white interior filler to fill in stencilled shapes. Why not make several matching frames using different combinations of motifs?

Leaf-stippled Frames

you will need

2 wooden frames, prepared and sanded

acrylic paint: dark green

paintbrush

fine-grade sandpaper (glasspaper)

paper

pencil

stencil card (card stock)

scissors

ready-mixed interior filler

stencil brush

1 Paint the frames dark green. When dry, gently rub them down to create a distressed effect. Enlarge the templates at the back of the book to fit the frames, transfer them to stencil card (card stock) and cut them out.

2 Position a stencil on one of the frames and stipple ready-mixed filler through it using a stencil brush. Reposition the stencil and repeat. Continue all round the frame, spacing the leaves evenly. Leave to dry.

3 Repeat with a different combination of motifs on the second frame. When the filler is completely hard, gently smooth the leaves with fine-grade sandpaper (glasspaper).

Three-dimensional motifs applied on the face of a picture frame are simple to create using interior filler. Tint the filler any colour you choose by adding pigment, gouache or watercolour paint.

Raised Motif Frame

you will need
bowls
gouache paint: cobalt blue
2.5cm/1in flat sable paintbrush
wooden frame, prepared and sanded
fine-grade sandpaper (glasspaper)
tracing paper
pencil
stencil card (card stock)
cutting mat
craft knife
interior filler
pigment
stencil brush

1 In a bowl, blend one part cobalt blue gouache paint with three parts water. Paint this wash on to the frame in long, even strokes, working from mitre to mitre. Leave to dry for approximately 15 minutes.

2 Lightly distress the face and edges of the frame by rubbing them with fine-grade sandpaper (glasspaper).

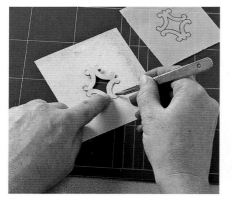

3 Trace the design for the frame using the template at the back of the book, then transfer on to stencil card (card stock). Place this on a cutting mat and cut out the design with a craft knife.

4 Mix two parts interior filler with one part water and mix to an ice cream consistency. Add pigment to tint the filler. Place the stencil on the frame and hold securely. Apply the filler by stippling with a stencil brush.

5 Lift off the stencil and repeat all round the frame. Leave the filler to dry for approximately 30 minutes, then lightly smooth the surface using fine-grade sandpaper.

This frame is made from an old plank sawn into pieces and simply glued together. The paint and stencil are applied and then rubbed back to produce an antique effect.

Framed Chalkboard

you will need

spray adhesive

stencil card (card stock)

craft knife and cutting mat

wooden frame, prepared and sanded

emulsion (latex) paint: blue and red

small paintbrush

medium-grade sandpaper (glasspaper)

artist's acrylic paint: black

stencil brush

antiquing varnish

varnish brush

hardboard, cut 2.5cm/1in larger all around than the inner frame measurement

chalkboard paint

hammer

panel pins (brads)

1 Photocopy the templates provided at the back of the book. Spray the back of each with adhesive and stick on to stencil card (card stock). Cut out the shapes.

2 Paint the frame with an even coat of blue emulsion (latex) paint. Leave the frame to dry.

4 Rub the paint with sandpaper (glasspaper) to reveal the grain of the wood.

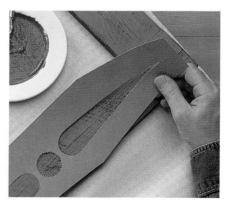

5 Spray the back of each stencil lightly with spray adhesive and place on the frame.

3 Paint the inner and outer edges of the frame red. Leave to dry.

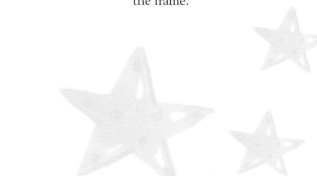

6 Darken the red paint by mixing in a little black acrylic paint. Using a stencil brush, stipple red paint through the stencils to produce an even covering of paint. Practise first on the wrong side of the frame if you are unfamiliar with the technique.

7 Using the stencil brush, rub the dark red paint deep into the grain in just a few places.

8 When dry, rub over with sandpaper (glasspaper) to remove any dark red paint from the surface.

9 Apply a coat of antiquing varnish. Leave to dry.

10 Paint the hardboard with two coats of chalkboard paint. Leave to dry. Fix the chalkboard to the back of the frame, using panel pins (brads).

Adorn an old gilded frame with gilded and coloured seashells to give it a baroque look. Shells are ideal objects for gilding, as the added lustre brings out their beautiful natural detail.

Gilded Shell Frame

you will need

assorted seashells

red oxide spray primer

1cm/½ in paintbrushes

water-based size

Dutch metal leaf: gold and aluminium

soft brush

amber shellac

acrylic varnish

acrylic paints: pale blue, pink and orange

soft cloths

gilded frame

strong clear glue

1 Spray the shells with an even coat of red oxide spray primer and leave to dry for 30–60 minutes. Paint on a thin, even coat of water-based size and leave for 20–30 minutes, until it becomes clear and tacky.

2 Gild the shells with gold or aluminium Dutch metal leaf, dabbing the leaf into place with a soft brush. Use the brush to remove any excess leaf.

3 Seal the gold shells with a thin, even coat of amber shellac and leave to dry for 45–60 minutes. Seal the aluminium-leaf covered shells with acrylic varnish and leave to dry for at least an hour.

4 Mix some pale blue acrylic paint with a little water. Paint on to the shells, then rub off most of the paint with a cloth, allowing only a little paint to remain in the recessed areas. Colour some of the shells in pink and orange. Leave to dry for 30 minutes.

5 Arrange the shells on the gilded frame and attach in place with strong clear glue. Leave to dry thoroughly before hanging the frame.

This distressed effect is achieved using a wax resist technique. The wax prevents the top coat of paint adhering in places, so that it can be rubbed away to reveal the second colour beneath.

Distressed Mirror Frame

you will need

mirror with wooden frame, prepared and sanded

masking tape

emulsion (latex) paint: white, light green and blue

paintbrush

soft cloth

wax polish

sandpaper (glasspaper)

1 Protect the mirror with masking tape. Paint the frame with white emulsion (latex) paint, then apply a coat of light green emulsion. Leave to dry.

2 Using a cloth, rub wax polish over the surface of the frame. Leave to dry. Paint a coat of blue emulsion paint over the frame and leave to dry.

3 When the paint is dry, rub sandpaper (glasspaper) over the whole surface to reveal some of the colour beneath. Remove the masking tape.

Faux verdigris is achieved by using green and metallic acrylic paints to simulate the green deposit that forms on copper or brass which has become oxidized after exposure to the elements.

Verdigris Frame

you will need
wooden frame, prepared and sanded
acrylic paint: iridescent copper, emerald
green, white and black
paintbrush
soft cloth

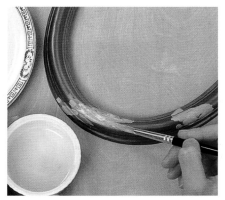

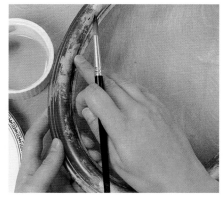

1 Paint the frame with iridescent copper acrylic paint. When dry, mix emerald green with white and paint in random patches on to the copper.

2 While the paint is wet, remove some of the green colour with a cloth, to create a textured look.

3 Paint on some small areas of black acrylic and rub the paint in with your fingers. Leave to dry.

Liming wax is usually applied to attractively grained wood such as oak or ash. The white pigment in the mixture settles into the grain of the wood, while the wax on the surface remains translucent.

Lime-waxed Frame

you will need

wooden frame, prepared and sanded

coarse- and fine-grade sandpaper (glasspaper)

liming wax

wire (steel) wool

cloth

1 Sand the frame all over, initially with coarse-grade then with fine-grade sandpaper, to give a smooth surface.

2 Pick up some liming wax on a piece of wire (steel) wool and apply it to the frame in long even strokes, continuing all around the frame. Work the wax into the wood grain as you go. Apply a second coat of liming wax to achieve a deeper effect.

3 When you have covered the frame completely, gently polish the liming wax with a cloth. Do not use excessive pressure as this will wipe off too much of the wax.

Woodstain penetrates the wood but allows the grain to show through, giving a translucent finish. Brushes should be cleaned with methylated spirits (denatured alcohol) when using a spirit-based stain.

Woodstained Frame

you will need
wooden frame, prepared and sanded
spirit (alcohol)-based woodstain
methylated spirits (denatured alcohol)
glass bowl
rubber (latex) gloves
2.5cm/1in flat sable paintbrush
acrylic varnish and brush

1 For an opaque result, use pure un-diluted woodstain. For a translucent finish, dilute the woodstain with methylated spirits (denatured alcohol). Decant the mixture into a glass bowl. Wear rubber (latex) gloves when working with woodstain.

2 Dip the paintbrush into the solution, wiping off the excess. Apply the stain, working from mitre to mitre, in a single long, even stroke. Repeat all around the sides of the frame. Leave to dry for 10–15 minutes. Two or three coats may be required.

3 When the woodstain is dry to the touch, apply a coat of acrylic varnish. Leave to dry before applying one or two more coats as required.

With the help of a template and tracing paper, you can handpaint a frame to look as good as if it was painted by an artist. Luscious grapes and vine leaves decorate this frame.

Painted Vine Mirror Frame

you will need
masking tape
wooden frame, prepared and sanded, with mirror
paintbrush
emulsion (latex) paint: white
pencil
tracing paper
coloured chalk
acrylic paint: purple, sap green, white and raw umber
artist's brushes
oak-coloured antique varnish
cloth

1 Stick masking tape around the edges of the mirror. Paint the frame with three coats of white emulsion (latex) paint. Trace the grape design provided at the back of the book. Rub chalk on to the back of the tracing. Place the design on a corner of the frame and go over the lines with the pencil, to transfer the design on to the frame. Repeat with the other corners.

2 Dilute the purple and green acrylic paints with water. Using a fine artist's brush, paint a wash of purple for the grapes and green for the leaves on the design. Add white highlights on the grapes and leaves.

3 Paint an outline around the fruit and leaves with raw umber paint using a very fine brush. When dry, apply a coat of antique varnish and rub off any excess with a cloth, to create an antiqued effect.

The uneven markings and crazing that occur naturally in marble can be imitated very convincingly by the skilful application of paint, using just a brush and a feather.

Marble-effect Mirror Frame

you will need

wooden frame, prepared and sanded, with mirror

masking tape

white eggshell paint

paintbrush

oil paint: raw umber, sap green and white

turpentine

linseed oil

cloth

goose feather

soft brush

1 Protect the mirror with masking tape and paint the frame with white eggshell. Thin raw umber and green paint with turpentine and linseed oil. Paint on the frame and take off the excess with a cloth for a textured look.

2 Dip the end of the feather into the green paint mixture and the white oil paint. Draw lines on the frame with the feather. Mix some paint in a stronger colour and draw more lines, varying the pressure of the feather.

3 While the paint is still damp, brush over the frame with a soft brush to merge the lines together, producing the marbled effect.

Transform a wooden frame into a gleaming gilded one using Dutch gold leaf, varnish and orange acrylic glaze. Flicking enamel varnish over the frame creates an effective antiqued look.

Good as Gold

you will need

wooden frame, prepared and sanded

red oxide spray primer

paintbrushes

water-based size

Dutch metal leaf: gold

soft brush

wire (steel) wool

methylated spirits (denatured alcohol)

clear shellac

old stiff brush

French enamel varnish

rubber (latex) gloves

acrylic paint: orange

soft cloth

1 Prime the wooden picture frame with the red oxide spray primer. (Use the spray in a well-ventilated room.) Obtain an even coverage and ensure that the wood is completely covered.

2 Apply a thin, but even, coat of water-based size, painting out any bubbles that appear. Leave the size to get tacky, following the manufacturer's instructions on the bottle of size.

3 Place sheets of metal leaf on the size, dabbing them into place with a soft brush. Work around the frame adding leaf, then fill in any tears or gaps.

4 When the surface is completely covered, remove any excess leaf with the soft brush. Using wire (steel) wool and methylated spirits (denatured alcohol), rub over the raised areas to reveal some of the base coat.

5 Apply a coat of shellac to seal the metal leaf and prevent tarnishing.

6 Dip an old, stiff brush into some French enamel varnish and, wearing rubber (latex) gloves, flick the bristles to spray enamel over the frame.

7 When the varnish is dry, dilute some orange acrylic paint with a little water to make a glaze. Paint the glaze all over the frame.

8 While the glaze is still wet, wipe off the excess with a soft cloth so that some paint remains in the detail areas. Allow to dry.

For this striking mirror frame, gold leaf was also used on the frame to create an unusual, unified design. In spite of the delicate appearance of real gold leaf, traditional oil gilding is very hardwearing.

Oil-gilded Frame

you will need

paintbrush
wooden frame, prepared and sanded
gouache paint: ultramarine
white chinagraph pencil
round oil paintbrush
oil size (half-hour drying time)
loose gold leaf
gilder's cushion
gilder's knife
gilder's tip
cotton wool (cotton balls)
soft paintbrush

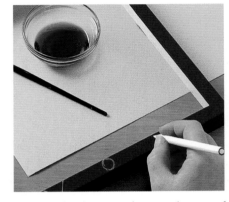

1 Paint the frame with several coats of ultramarine gouache, allowing each coat to dry completely before applying the next. Draw the design on the frame using a white chinagraph pencil.

2 Using a round oil paintbrush, apply the oil size to the marked shapes. Leave the size to dry for 15–20 minutes, following the manufacturer's instructions, until slightly tacky.

3 Place the gold leaf on a gilder's cushion and cut it into pieces of the appropriate size using a gilder's knife. Brush a gilder's tip over the side of your face to pick up a little grease, then pick up the gold leaf with the tip.

4 Carefully place the gold leaf on the oil-sized design. Leave to dry for another 20 minutes, then gently press the gold leaf down with a pad of cotton wool (cotton ball).

5 After 15–20 minutes, gently wipe off the excess gold leaf with a soft paintbrush or a small pad of cotton wool (cotton ball).

Beautiful old frames can often be found in junk shops, but are usually in need of some restoration. You can restore a frame to its former glory using cold-curing silicone rubber to make a mould for missing details.

Frame Restoration

you will need

damaged gilded frame, cleaned

cold-curing silicone base

curing agent

plastic container

spoon

small spatula

bag of sand

casting plaster

small plastic pot

craft knife

2-part epoxy resin glue

2-part epoxy putty

artist's paintbrush

emulsion (latex) paint: red

picture framer's gilt wax

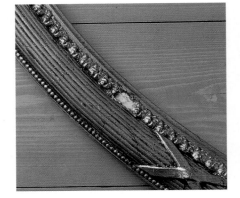

1 A small area on this frame is missing. Because it is intricately moulded it needs to be copied exactly in order to blend in with the rest of the frame.

2 Mix the cold-curing silicone (see Techniques) and spread a thick coat on to an identical area that is clean and not damaged. Remove when dry.

4 Remove the cast from the mould and use a craft knife to cut it to the right size to fit the missing area. Stick it to the frame with epoxy resin glue, then leave to dry for 24 hours. Fill any gaps between the cast and the frame with two-part epoxy putty, using a small spatula. Leave to dry for 2 hours.

5 Using an artist's paintbrush, paint the repaired area with red emulsion (latex) paint. Repeat if the plaster is not completely covered by the first coat. Leave to dry for 3 hours. Dip your finger in gilt wax and gently rub it over the red paint. Blend it in carefully at the edges of the repair to match the existing gilding.

3 Support the rubber mould on a bag loosely filled with sand. Mix a small amount of plaster in a plastic pot (see Techniques) and pour the plaster into the mould. When it is full, shake it slightly to allow any air bubbles to rise. Leave to dry for 2 hours.

6 Glue the cork support to the centre of the cardboard. This will act as a backing board.

7 Apply two coats of white emulsion (latex) paint to the front of the frame and the backing board, allowing each to dry before applying the next.

8 Take up a little green paint on a dry brush and lightly brush over the frame to leave a trace of paint on the surface.

9 Using an artist's paintbrush, colour the inside and outside edges of the frame with dark blue acrylic paint.

10 Glue the scabious flowerhead to the cork support in the centre of the backing board.

11 Centre the frame over the backing board and hold in place with strips of double-sided adhesive tape.

This modern picture frame is decorated using a simple stencilling technique and treated with a crackle glaze. The brightly coloured paintwork is distressed slightly to give a very attractive finish.

Crackle-glaze Picture Frame

you will need

wooden frame, prepared and sanded

emulsion (latex) paint: yellow ochre,
turquoise, orange, lime green
and bright pink

paintbrushes

acrylic crackle glaze

masking tape

craft knife

flat artist's paintbrush

coarse-grade sandpaper (glasspaper)

acrylic varnish and brush

1 Paint the frame with two coats of yellow ochre emulsion (latex) paint, allowing each to dry. Brush on a coat of crackle glaze. Leave to dry according to the manufacturer's instructions.

2 Place strips of masking tape in a pattern on two opposite sides of the frame, using the finished photograph as your guide.

3 Where the ends of the tape overlap, carefully trim off the excess with a craft knife to leave a straight edge.

4 Brush turquoise paint on some unmasked sections of the frame, working in one direction. The crackle effect will appear almost immediately.

5 Brush orange paint on alternate sections of the pattern in the same way. Paint the remaining sections lime green. Leave the paint to dry, and then carefully peel away the masking tape.

6 Using a flat artist's paintbrush, apply bright pink paint to the areas that were covered by the masking tape. Do this freehand to give the frame a hand-painted look. Leave to dry.

7 Rub coarse-grade sandpaper (glasspaper) over the crackled paint surface to reveal some of the yellow ochre paint beneath.

8 Seal the frame with two coats of acrylic varnish. Apply the first coat quickly, taking care not to overbrush and reactivate the crackle glaze.

A craquelure effect is created using two varnishes. One is slow-drying, while the other is fast-drying. As the slow-drying lower layer contracts it causes cracking in the dry layer of varnish above.

Craquelure Frame

you will need

2.5cm/1in flat sable paintbrush

gouache paint: white

wooden frame, prepared and sanded

fine-grade sandpaper (glasspaper)

clear spray lacquer

2.5cm/1in flat oil paintbrush

two-stage crackle varnish

cloths

palette or plate

oil paint: olive green

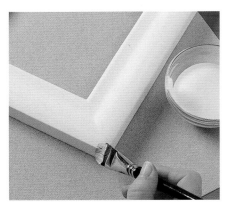

1 With a flat sable paintbrush, apply four coats of white gouache paint to the frame, allowing each to dry before applying the next. Rub over the frame with sandpaper (glasspaper). Spray with clear spray lacquer to make the surface less absorbent.

2 Using a flat oil paintbrush, apply a coat of stage-1 crackle varnish sparingly over the frame. When the varnish has become slightly tacky, apply the stage-2 crackle glaze. Cracks should begin to appear in about an hour. Leave the frame to dry overnight.

3 Wrap your finger in a cloth and dip it into olive green oil paint. Apply the paint all over the frame, working the colour into the cracks. Then wipe the paint off with a cloth; this will remove paint from the surface but leave the colour in the cracks.

Verre eglomisé is glass that has been mirrored using gold or silver leaf, creating a magical, mysterious effect. The technique is named after an eighteenth-century art dealer, Jean-Baptiste Glomy.

Verre Eglomisé Frame

you will need
2.5cm/1in flat oil paintbrush
rubber (latex) gloves
metal polish
wooden frame, prepared and sanded
sponge
black patina
burnishing tool
glass to fit frame
cloths
methylated spirits (denatured alcohol)
gelatine capsules
glass bowl
deep tray
white gold leaf (loose)
gilder's knife
gilder's cushion
2.5cm/1in flat sable paintbrush
gilder's tip
kettle
cotton wool (cotton balls)
pumice powder (0003 grade)
safety mask
black lacquer spray

1 Using a flat oil paintbrush and wearing rubber (latex) gloves, apply metal polish to the frame. Dab the sponge over the polish as you work along the frame for a textured finish. Leave for 30 minutes. Apply a second layer in the same way. Leave overnight to dry.

2 Apply a coat of black patina over the frame, wiping it off as you work. The patina will remain in the recessed areas, giving the impression of age. Leave the frame to dry overnight.

3 Polish the frame with a burnishing tool to give a soft sheen.

4 To create the mirror, clean the glass thoroughly to remove all dirt and grease, using a cloth dipped in methylated spirits (denatured alcohol). ▶

5 Place half a gelatine capsule in a glass bowl and add a little boiling water. When the capsule has completely dissolved, add 300ml/½ pint/1¼ cups cold water.

6 Place the glass at an angle of 45° in a deep tray, so that the solution can run down freely. Cut the gold leaf into small squares with a gilder's knife. Using a flat sable paintbrush, apply the solution to the glass and immediately lay a piece of gold leaf on the solution using a gilder's tip.

7 Work from the top to the bottom of the glass. Continue until you have gilded the entire glass, then leave to dry. When the gold leaf looks shiny, it is dry. If it is matt, it is not yet dry.

8 To seal the leaf, hold the gilded glass approximately 20–25cm/8–10in away from the steam of a boiling kettle. Leave to dry. Once dry, gently brush off any excess leaf with cotton wool (cotton balls).

9 A more distressed, antiqued look can be achieved by gently rubbing pumice powder into the gold leaf with your fingertips. When the desired effect has been achieved, brush away the excess powder.

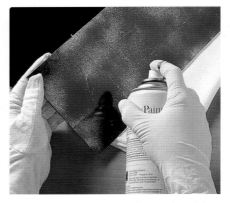

10 Wearing a mask and rubber (latex) gloves, spray black lacquer over the gilded side of the glass. Hold the spray about 20–25cm/8–10in away for an even coat. Leave to dry. Insert the gilded glass in the frame.

This lovely antique-looking mirror, with its intricately moulded frame, has been decorated using the water gilding technique. The delicate finish of this type of gilding is created by building up layers of gesso.

Water-gilded Frame

you will need

ready-made acrylic gesso: white
and red
bain marie or double boiler
wooden frame, cleaned
assorted paintbrushes
water-based size
loose gold leaf
gilder's cushion
gilder's tip
petroleum jelly, optional
cotton wool (cotton balls)
soft brush
agate burnisher
wire (steel) wool
cotton rag
clear shellac
string
soft cloth, optional

1 Heat the ready-made white gesso in a bain marie or double boiler for 5 minutes. Paint a coat of gesso on to the picture frame and leave to harden for 1–2 hours.

2 Heat the ready-made red gesso in the same way and paint up to eight thin coats of gesso on to the frame, leaving each coat to dry for 1–2 hours before applying the next one.

3 Paint a thin, even coat of water-based size over the frame and leave for 20–30 minutes until it becomes clear and tacky. Always follow the manufacturer's instructions.

4 Blow a sheet of gold leaf on to a gilder's cushion. Brush a gilder's tip over the side of your face to pick up a little grease, or smear a little petroleum jelly on your arm and brush the tip over it. Touch the tip to the gold leaf to pick up the whole sheet.

5 Lay the leaf on the frame and gently press into place with cotton wool (cotton balls). Repeat until the whole frame is covered.

6 Remove any excess leaf with a soft brush. Leave for 24 hours then burnish the gilding with an agate burnisher. Take care not to rub too hard in case you damage the gesso.

7 To create a distressed effect, gently rub the raised areas with wire (steel) wool to remove a little of the leaf. Take care not to rub too hard.

◄ **8** Make a polishing rubber by wrapping some cotton wool (cotton balls) in a clean rag. Before tying the rag, pour in a little clear shellac to soak the cotton. Tie up the rag with string and, when the shellac soaks through the rag, rub it over the gilding. The surface can be buffed with a soft cloth when dry.

Penwork was one of many artistic amusements popular at the end of the eighteenth century. This elaborately detailed black decoration is traced from a copyright-free book on to a white frame using black ink.

Ink Penwork Frame

you will need
paintbrushes
acrylic gesso
wooden frame, prepared and sanded
medium- and fine-grade sandpaper
(glasspaper)
white acrylic paint
tracing paper
design
masking tape
hard and soft pencils
fine black marker pen
emulsion (latex) paint: black
safety mask
clear spray lacquer
2.5cm/1in flat lacquer brush
shellac

1 Apply four coats of acrylic gesso to the frame, allowing it to dry between layers. Sand the gesso with medium-, then fine-grade sandpaper (glasspaper). Apply four layers of white paint to the frame, allowing each coat to dry for 5–10 minutes before applying the next. Place tracing paper over the design. Hold in place with masking tape and trace with a soft pencil.

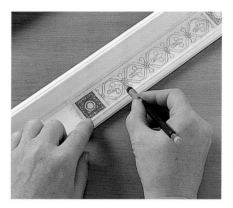

2 Place the tracing, pencil-side down, on the frame, and secure with masking tape. Using a hard pencil, draw over the design. This will transfer the pencil design on to the frame.

3 Remove the tracing paper and ink over the design with a fine black marker pen. Paint the rebate with black emulsion (latex) paint.

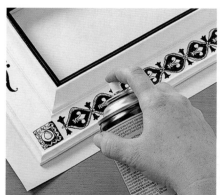

4 When the penwork is completed, spray clear lacquer over the frame to seal it. Wear a safety mask and hold the can approximately 20–25cm/ 8–10in from the frame. Leave to dry.

5 Using a flat lacquer brush, apply four layers of shellac to the frame, allowing each coat to dry for about 30 minutes before applying the next. This will give an aged, ivory appearance.

This technique involves burning a design into a frame with a heat gun. A close-grained wood, such as oak or ash, is recommended to stop the design spreading. Polish the frame with tinted wax to finish.

Scorched Frame

you will need
kitchen foil
white chinagraph pencil
craft knife or tin snips
oak or ash frame
heat gun
safety gloves
coarse- and fine-grade sandpaper
(glasspaper)
raw sienna pigment
clear wax
soft cloths

1 Draw your design on foil using a white chinagraph pencil. Cut out the design using a craft knife or tin snips. Place the foil template on the bare frame. Using a heat gun and wearing safety gloves, scorch the design into the wood, holding the gun 10–15cm/ 4–6in away from the wood.

2 Using coarse-grade sandpaper (glasspaper), sand off any over-burns. Repeat with fine-grade sandpaper.

3 Mix raw sienna pigment with wax in the proportion of 1.5ml/¼tsp of pigment to 15ml/1 tbsp of clear wax.

4 Apply the pigmented wax to the frame using a soft cloth. Work all around the frame.

5 Using a dry, clean cloth, polish up the wax to a soft sheen.

Tortoiseshell was popular in the eighteenth century, for hairbrush backs, trinket boxes and frames. This traditional technique, using pigments suspended in shellac over gilding, produces a realistic and effective imitation.

Tortoiseshell-effect Frame

you will need

oil paint: yellow ochre

2.5cm/1in flat oil paintbrush

wooden frame, prepared and sanded

oil size (half-hour drying time)

loose gold leaf

gilder's cushion

gilder's knife

gilder's tip

cotton wool (cotton balls)

2.5cm/1in lacquer paintbrush

pure shellac

palette or plate

pigments: yellow ochre, burnt sienna, Venetian red and burnt umber

round sable paintbrush

fine-grade wet-and-dry paper

white spirit (paint thinner)

cloths

metal polish

1 Apply yellow ochre oil paint all over the frame, and leave to dry overnight. Apply another coat and allow to dry overnight again. Apply oil size over the face and outer edges of the frame using the flat oil brush. Leave to dry for 15 minutes. When slightly tacky, begin to apply the gold leaf.

2 Place the leaf on the gilder's cushion and cut it into pieces. Brush the gilder's tip on the side of your face to pick up a little grease. Place the tip on the gold leaf and pick it up vertically. Place it on a sized section of the frame, without letting the tip touch the frame, then lift the tip up vertically. Repeat all around the frame.

3 Once the whole frame is gilded, let it dry for 20 minutes. Gently tamp down the gold leaf with cotton wool (cotton balls). Leave to dry overnight.

4 Using a lacquer brush, apply four layers of pure shellac over the frame, allowing each layer to dry for 30 minutes before applying the next. ▶

5 Mix 30ml/2 tbsp of shellac with 1.5ml/¼ tsp of yellow ochre pigment, using a round sable paintbrush. Paint this mixture on to the frame using diagonal strokes, leaving gaps for the rest of the pigments.

6 Repeat step 4. Then repeat step 5, replacing the yellow ochre pigment with burnt sienna. Apply another four layers of shellac, again allowing each to dry for 30 minutes before applying the next coat.

7 Repeat step 6 using Venetian red pigment. Apply another four layers of shellac, allowing each coat to dry completely before applying the next.

8 Repeat step 6, using burnt umber pigment. Apply eight layers of shellac, allowing each layer to dry completely before applying the next. Leave overnight.

9 When the shellac is touch dry, dip fine-grade wet-and-dry paper into a bowl of white spirit (paint thinner) and rub very gently all around the frame, ensuring that the wet-and-dry paper is saturated with white spirit. Be careful not to rub through to the pigmented layers.

10 Wipe off excess white spirit with a cloth. Then apply a small amount of metal polish and polish with another cloth to produce a smooth and shiny finish. Finally, polish the entire frame with a fresh clean cloth.

This Javanese wax-resist technique is traditionally used to produce vibrant designs in dyed fabric, but here it makes a subtle and delicate pattern on a smooth wooden picture frame.

Batik Frame

you will need

untreated wooden free-standing frame

pencil

tracing paper

ruler

general-purpose wax

wax pot or double boiler

canting

paintbrushes

woodstains: willow, mahogany and olive-green

masking tape

stencil brush (short-haired)

eraser, optional

hairdryer

cloth

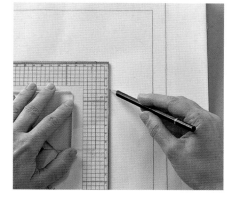

1 Draw around the frame on to a piece of tracing paper and work out the design to scale, or enlarge the template provided at the back of the book. Allow for a narrow border on the inside and outside edges. Using a ruler, draw the borders on all the edges of the frame.

2 Heat the wax in a wax pot or double boiler. Wax in the ruled lines with a canting. Make sure there are no breaks in the line; the wax should stick firmly to the surface of the wood. If it brushes away easily, it is not hot enough.

3 Paint the borders with a rust-coloured woodstain, such as willow. Leave the frame to dry thoroughly.

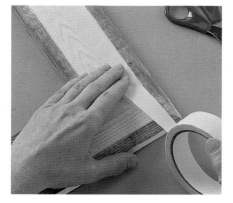

4 Stick masking tape around the edge of the borders to protect the central frame area. ▶

5 Use a stubby stencil brush to dab wax on to the frame borders. Do not apply too much wax, as some wood must be left free of wax so that more colours can be applied.

6 Remove the masking tape. Over-paint the waxed borders with a mahogany woodstain and leave to dry completely.

7 Place the design on top of the frame and trace the leaf pattern. The pencil marks on the wood should be as light as possible. If necessary, use an eraser to remove some of the pencil.

8 Wax in the leaf design with a canting, blocking in the leaves with wax. Once again, make sure that the wax is hot enough to stick firmly to the surface of the wood.

9 Over-paint the leaf design and central area of the frame with olive-green woodstain and leave to dry.

10 When the frame is dry, heat the wax with a hairdryer until it becomes molten. Rub the molten wax into the surface of the wood with a rag. Try to spread the wax as much as possible across the surface of the frame, as this will help to bring out the colours of the woodstain.

Cardboard, Tin, Wire and Paper

You can make unusual and innovative frames from the most basic materials, and in many cases you need look no further than paper and cardboard. Cardboard is strong enough to form a rigid structure, which can then be inventively decorated with paper or paint. Use coils of galvanized wire for intricate frame edgings, or stamp sheet metal with a nail or centre punch to make decorative embossed patterns in both traditional and modern styles.

Wire   Coils are probably the most commonly used decorative devices in wire-work. They also have a practical use as they neaten and make safe what would otherwise be sharp ends, while adding grace and style.

Closed coils

Using round-nosed (snub-nosed) pliers, make a small loop at the end of the wire. Hold the loop firmly with parallel (channel-type) pliers, and use them to bend the wire around until you have a coil of the size required.

Open coils

Using round-nosed (snub-nosed) pliers, make a small loop at the end of the wire. Holding the loop in the pliers, place your thumb against the wire and draw the wire across it to form a curve. Use your eye to judge the space left between the rings of the coil. Finally, flatten the coil.

Flattened extended coils

1 Wrap the wire several times around a broomstick or other cylindrical object to make a coil. If you are using galvanized wire, you will need to brace your thumb firmly against it.

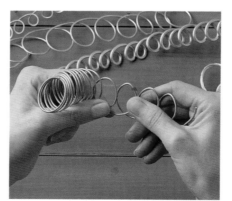

2 After removing the coil from the broomstick, splay out the loops one by one, holding them firmly between your fingers and thumbs.

Safety advice

• A heavy work shirt and protective leather gloves should always be worn when handling either cut metal pieces or uncut sheet metal.

• Tin shears and snips are strong enough to cut through fairly heavy metal, and are very sharp. They should be handled with respect and, like all other tools, should always be kept in a safe place, well away from children, both during and after use.

• Clean up as you work. Collect small shards of tin together as you cut and make sure you don't leave any on the floor where people and animals might walk on them.

• A protective face mask and goggles should be worn during soldering as the hot metal, solder and flux give off fumes. Work should be carried out on a soldering mat and the iron placed on a metal rest when not in use.

• Soldering should always be carried out in a well-ventilated area. Don't lean too near your work during soldering to avoid close contact with fumes.

• Wear protective gloves when soldering, as the soldering iron and metal tend to get very hot.

Metal Punching is one of the most common methods of decorating tin. A centre punch or nail, plus a ball hammer, are used to produce the knobbly patterns, either on the front or back of the tin.

Getting the design right

If you want to emboss a sophisticated pattern, draw the design out first on a sheet of graph paper and punch through the paper into the tin, following the lines. The graph paper should be taped to the tin, and the tin attached to a piece of chipboard using panel pins (brads) to keep it steady as you punch.

Punching tin from the front

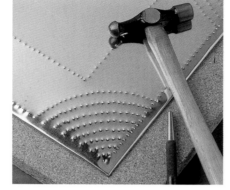

If a design is punched into tin from the front, the resulting pattern will be indented. If it is punched from the back, the pattern will be raised. If an area of tin is punched from the front, and the indentations are made very close together, the punched area recedes and the unpunched area becomes slightly raised.

Punching tin from the back

Punching a pattern into a piece of tin from the back leaves a very pleasing knobbly effect on the surface of the tin. Patterns can be applied with punches or nails of different sizes to make a dotty texture. Short lines can be made using a small chisel. It is also possible to buy decorative punches that have designs engraved on the tip.

Embossing aluminium foil

Aluminium foil can easily be cut and folded, so it is useful for cladding frames. Its softness makes it very easy to emboss by drawing on to the back of the foil using an empty ballpoint pen, which produces a raised design on the other side.

Cutting tin

If you are cutting a small intricate shape from sheet tin, tin snips are easier to manage than shears. Don't attempt to turn the snips around in the metal: cut as far as you can, then remove the snips and turn the metal before continuing.

Corrugated paper can look stunning when used innovatively. It is easy to work with but crushes easily. To avoid this problem and create a different look, flatten the ridges with a ruler before you begin work.

Corrugated Picture Frame

you will need
metal ruler
pencil
corrugated cardboard
craft knife
cutting mat
fine corrugated paper in
different colours
scissors
PVA (white) glue and brush

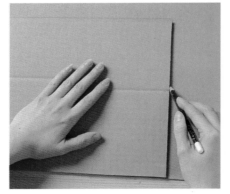

1 Measure the image to be framed and decide on the size and shape of frame required. Draw the frame backing on to corrugated coardboard and cut it out using a craft knife and metal ruler.

2 Use the backing as a template to draw and cut out the front of the frame from coloured corrugated paper. Using the image as a guide, mark and carefully cut out the central frame area.

3 Make a stand for the frame from cardboard and glue in place on the back. Decorate the front with twisted strips of coloured paper. Glue the image in place so that the backing colour shows through in a thin border all round. Stick the frame together.

Plain brown parcel wrap is an ideal material for papier mâché, and its warm tones produce a stylish, natural look. This frame, with its low-relief pattern, exploits the material's qualities in a simple design.

Starry Cardboard Frame

you will need
metal ruler
T-square
pencil
thick corrugated cardboard
cutting mat
craft knife
tracing paper
strong, clear glue
lightweight corrugated cardboard
PVA (white) glue
paintbrush
sheet of plastic
brown parcel wrap
masking tape
picture hanger

1 From thick corrugated cardboard cut a 38cm/15in square for the frame. Cut out an 18cm/7in square from the centre. Cut out eight stars using the template provided, and four circles from cardboard. Glue the circles to four stars. Glue the stars to the frame. Put the plain ones at the corners.

2 Cut a backing board and a frame spacer from lightweight cardboard. Prime all the pieces with diluted PVA (white) glue. Leave to dry. Glue the spacer to the back of the frame. Tear wide strips of brown paper and dip them into the diluted glue. Cover the frame and backing with two layers.

3 When the papier mâché is dry, glue the covered backing board to the frame, lining up the edges accurately. Hold the frame together with masking tape and seal the bottom and side edges with two layers of papier mâché strips. When dry, glue a hanger to the back with clear glue.

Decorated with glass droplets, this marine-inspired mirror is made of moulded papier mâché. The wave-like frame is cut from cardboard, then covered with paper pulp to build up its organic form.

Seaside Papier Mâché Mirror

you will need
strong cardboard
craft knife
cutting mat
newspaper
wallpaper paste
PVA (white) glue and brush
paintbrush
acrylic primer: white
glass droplets
epoxy resin glue
gouache paints: deep yellow, cadmium yellow, deep cobalt, pale blue, green, red, indigo and white
artist's paintbrushes
enamel paint: gold
clear gloss and matt varnishes
mirror and fixing tabs
plate-hanging fixture
screwdriver

Papier mâché pulp (see Techniques)
newspaper
2 tablespoons PVA (white) glue
1 tablespoon linseed oil
few drops oil of cloves
2 tablespoons wallpaper paste

1 Enlarge the template at the back of the book on a photocopier. Transfer it to the cardboard and cut out using a craft knife and working on a cutting mat. Make the paper pulp by mixing all the ingredients together and apply this to the cardboard, to build up a three-dimensional form. Allow to dry.

2 Cover the whole frame with three to four layers of newspaper, soaked in wallpaper paste. Allow to dry. Coat with PVA (white) glue, then with acrylic primer. When this is dry, attach the glass droplets using epoxy resin glue. Decorate with gouache paints and add detail with the gold paint.

3 Paint the frame with several coats of gloss varnish, adding matt varnish in places to provide contrast. Allow the varnish to dry between each coat. Secure the mirror with mirror fixing-tabs. Finally, attach the plate-hanging fixture, securing all screws with epoxy resin glue.

This delicate frame is created using a plastic light switch surround as a mould. The mottled cream pulp is made from two shades of scrap paper and is applied to create a deliberately irregular shape.

Hammered Paper Frame

you will need

white and cream paper scraps

liquidizer

sieve

cloth

plastic light switch plate

cream or pearl beads

spoon

sponge

small hammer

PVA (white) glue

container for diluting glue

glue brush

tea or brown watercolour paint

artist's paintbrush

1 Mixing both colours of paper, make the scrap paper into pulp (see Techniques). Drain it through a sieve and squeeze out the excess moisture.

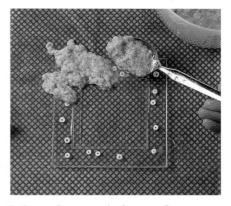

2 Smooth out a cloth on a flat waterproof surface, then put the light switch plate face down on top. Arrange the beads randomly on the plastic surface. Spoon pulp over the beads and the light switch plate, allowing it to spread over the edges of the plate. Sponge the pulp gently to remove any excess water.

3 Press a small hammer randomly into the wet pulp to make a textured border. Leave to dry, then remove the mould. Seal with diluted PVA (white) glue (equal parts glue and water). For an antique effect, stain the frame with tea or brown watercolour paint.

This sumptuous frame is achieved by applying ornate decoupage on top of Dutch metal leaf. Artful distressing gives the gold an antique look and lends a classical touch to a favourite piece.

Gilded Decoupage Mirror

you will need

wooden frame, prepared and sanded, with mirror

paintbrushes

acrylic primer

sandpaper (glasspaper)

emulsion (latex) paint: red

water-based size

scissors

Dutch metal leaf: gold

bronze powder, optional

fine artist's brush

soft brush

fine-grade wire (steel) wool

paper towels

white spirit (paint thinner)

shellac or sanding sealer

border motif

methylated spirits (denatured alcohol)

metal ruler

pencil

PVA (white) glue and brush

craft knife

water-based varnish

1 Apply a coat of acrylic primer to the frame. Leave to dry. Sand the surface. Apply two coats of red emulsion (latex) paint, sanding between coats to achieve a smooth finish. Brush on a thin coat of water-based size and leave until it begins to get slightly tacky.

2 Beginning with the flat areas of the frame, cut pieces of metal leaf to fit, making them slightly larger than required. Lay them on the frame, over-lapping each one. Smooth them down with your fingers, then remove the paper backing. Repeat until all the flat areas are covered.

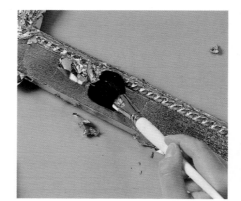

3 Cut strips of leaf to fit the raised areas. Press into place, using the leaf backing paper. For any missed areas, dab on a little bronze powder using a fine brush. Leave to dry overnight. Using a soft brush, remove the surplus leaf with a circular motion.

4 Gently rub the raised areas and edges of the frame with fine-grade wire (steel) wool to distress it. Moisten a piece of paper towel with white spirit (paint thinner) and clean off the dust left by the wire wool.

5 Seal the leaf with a coat of shellac or sanding sealer.

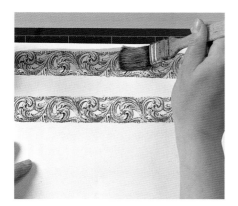

6 Estimate how the border motif will fit around the frame, and how many joins you need to make. Photocopy the required number of borders, adjusting the size if necessary. Seal and antique the borders using a little sanding sealer tinted with a little shellac, and mixed with a little methylated spirits (denatured alcohol).

7 Cut out the borders, starting with the centre of the design, then cut round the outer edges.

8 Using a metal ruler, find the centre point of the frame and mark lightly with a pencil. Take the first border, centre it and glue to hold the middle in place while you position the rest.

9 Accurately mitre the corners. Remove the loose pieces and stick down the remaining edges. Leave to dry thoroughly. To finish the frame and protect the gilding, apply five to ten coats of water-based varnish.

This striking papier mâché frame is decorated with decoupage motifs of oranges and lemons. Hunt around for interesting wrapping paper with suitable images.

Oranges and Lemons Decoupage

you will need
corrugated cardboard
craft knife
metal ruler
cutting mat
mirror, 15 x 18cm/6 x 7in
wallpaper paste
paintbrushes
newspaper
acrylic paints: black, yellow and green
artist's brush
paperclip (paper fastener)
acrylic gesso
natural sponge
wrapping paper
scraps of printed paper or manuscript
white tissue paper
matt acrylic varnish

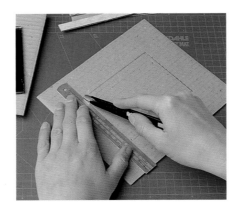

1 Cut two 17 x 20cm/6½ x 8in rectangles from corrugated cardboard using a craft knife and metal ruler and working on a cutting mat. Centre the mirror on one piece and cut spacer strips of cardboard to fit around it down two sides and across the bottom. Cut a window out of the centre of the other rectangle of cardboard, leaving a 4cm/1½ in border.

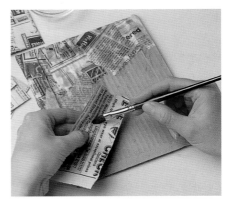

2 Coat all the pieces of cardboard with wallpaper paste. Leave to dry. Tear the newspaper into strips and coat them with paste. Cover the front of the frame with the newspaper. Paste the spacer strips in position on the sides and bottom of the back panel. Cover with papier mâché strips and leave to dry. Apply a second layer.

3 When the papier mâché is dry, paint the inside surfaces of the frame black to minimize any possible reflection they might give in the mirror.

4 Open out the paperclip (paper fastener) and thread one end through the papier mâché at the centre back of the frame. Paste strips of newspaper over the clip, leaving the top section showing to act as a hook.

5 Join the front of the frame to the back with more strips of pasted newspaper. For added strength, paste folded strips over the top of the frame to each side of the opening. Once dry, paint the frame with acrylic gesso.

6 Sponge the entire frame with thin yellow paint, then with green paint to create an all-over mottled effect.

7 Tear the motifs from the wrapping paper in interesting shapes and arrange them over the frame surface. Fill the gaps between the motifs with small pieces of printed paper. Paste in position.

8 Soften the design by tearing small pieces of white tissue paper and pasting them on to the frame. When the paste is dry, paint the frame with two coats of matt varnish and insert the mirror into the top slit to finish.

A plain mirror frame made from medium density fibreboard becomes a work of art when decorated with strips of wrapping paper. Apply crackle varnish and gold powder to give the frame a rich surface texture.

Swirly Mirror

you will need
mirror tile
pencil
medium density fibreboard (MDF),
8mm/⅓in thick
metal ruler
jigsaw
protective mask
wood glue
wrapping paper
craft knife
cutting mat
PVA (white) glue
felt-tipped pen
spray adhesive
two-stage crackle varnish
paintbrushes
gold powder
soft cloth
spray fixative
clear oil-based varnish
drill with wood drill bits
string
adhesive fixer pads
picture rings and chain
screwdriver

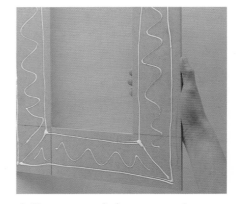

1 Draw around the mirror tile on to medium density fibreboard (MDF) and add a 9cm/3½in border all around. Wearing a mask, cut a back and a front panel to this size using a jigsaw. Cut out the centre of the front panel. Cut a plaque measuring 8.5 x 18cm/3¼ x 7in. Glue the panels together using wood glue.

2 Cut strips of wrapping paper in varying widths using a craft knife, ruler and cutting mat and arrange them on the frame front. Glue in place using PVA (white) glue.

3 To cover the corners, place a piece of wrapping paper on the frame and press around the edges. Remove and cut away the corner section. Glue the corner in place.

4 Using the template provided, draw two decorative swirls on the back of another paper using a felt-tipped pen. Cut out the swirls and spray the back of each with adhesive. Glue on to two corners of the frame.

5 Apply two thin coats of crackle varnish, following the manufacturer's instructions to give a craquelure finish to the frame.

6 Rub gold powder into the cracks with a cloth, using small amounts at a time. Rub off any excess. Seal the frame with fixative. Decorate the hanging plaque in the same way as the frame. Coat both the frame and the hanging plaque with varnish.

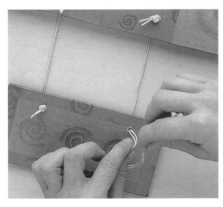

7 Drill two holes in the bottom of the frame and in the top of the hanging plaque. Join together with string.

8 Stick the mirror in place using adhesive fixer pads.

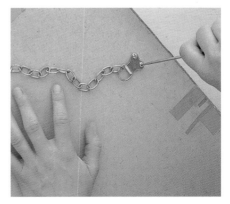

9 Attach the picture rings and chain to the back of the frame.

This attractive decoupage frame makes use of black and white photocopies of images, which are then coloured with paint. The shellac lends an antique colour to the frame.

Decoupage Frame

you will need

2.5cm/1in flat sable paintbrush

acrylic gesso

wooden frame, prepared and sanded

fine-grade sandpaper
(glasspaper)

yellow ochre pigment

photocopied designs

craft knife

cutting mat

round sable paintbrush

watercolour paints

PVA (white) glue

spray lacquer

2.5cm/1in lacquer paintbrush

shellac

white spirit (paint thinner)

fine and extra-fine wet-and-dry
paper

cork sanding block, optional

soft cloths

metal polish

1 Using a flat sable paintbrush, apply acrylic gesso over the frame. Allow to dry, then apply another four coats of gesso, allowing each coat to dry before applying the next. Allow to dry. Gently sand the surface with fine-grade sandpaper (glasspaper).

2 Combine 1.5ml/¼ tsp yellow ochre pigment with 30ml/2 tbsp water and blend thoroughly until no flecks of pigment are visible in the mixture. Using the flat sable paintbrush, apply two coats of the mixture over the frame. Allow to dry.

3 Photocopy the designs you wish to use from a book or magazine. Accurately cut out each shape with a craft knife, working on a cutting mat.

4 Using a round sable paintbrush, paint the photocopies with watercolour paints.

5 Glue the photocopied cut-outs to the frame using PVA (white) glue. Press them down carefully to remove air bubbles. Leave to dry.

6 Apply a coat of spray lacquer over the cut-outs. This will stop the paint on the photocopies bleeding into the coloured frame. Leave to dry.

7 Use a lacquer brush to apply ten coats of shellac to the frame, allowing each to dry before applying the next. Once the shellac is completely dry, rub the frame down with white spirit (paint thinner). Use wet-and-dry paper and a cork sanding block if the frame is flat, and finish with a finer wet-and-dry paper. Wipe off excess white spirit with a dry cloth. Apply a pea-sized amount of metal polish to a cloth and polish all around the frame. Buff up with a clean dry cloth.

Although this design looks handpainted, it is in fact created using motifs cut from paper table napkins. Classical borders and creamy white flowers combine with the ivy to decorate a very elegant frame.

Ivy Leaf Frame

you will need

masking tape

wooden frame, prepared and sanded, with oval mirror

paintbrushes

primer: white

emulsion (latex) paint: white

black-and-white paper borders

small scissors

wallpaper paste

pasting brush

white paper napkins with ivy leaf design

scissors

cream or white floral motifs

water-based varnish

two-step crackle varnish

hairdryer, optional

oil paint: raw umber

soft white cloths

white spirit (paint thinner)

oil-based varnish

1 Place masking tape around the edge of the mirror glass to protect it. Apply two coats of primer to the frame, followed by a coat of white emulsion (latex) paint. Allow the paint to dry between each coat.

2 Using a copyright-free border design, photocopy and cut out enough lengths to go round the outer and inner edges of the frame. Using wallpaper paste, apply the borders to the frame in small sections, aligning and joining up the design as necessary.

3 Remove the second, unprinted layer of tissue from the back of each napkin. Cut around the ivy shapes, leaving a narrow border of plain tissue.

4 Cut out floral motifs in the same way. Apply more paste to the mirror frame and stick the ivy trails and flowers in place. Allow to dry.

5 Apply several coats of water-based varnish to protect the design. Leave to dry between each coat. Following the manufacturer's instructions, brush on a thin, even layer of the first stage of the crackle varnish. Leave for 1–3 hours until tacky.

6 Brush on two coats of the second stage of the varnish, the second coat 30 minutes after the first, and leave to dry completely. If necessary, encourage the cracks to appear by moving a hairdryer, on its lowest setting, over the varnished surface.

7 Apply a small quantity of raw umber paint to a soft cloth. Add a little white spirit (paint thinner). Apply to the frame using a circular motion then, with a clean cloth, rub over the surface to remove the excess paint. The colour will remain in the cracks. Apply six to ten coats of oil-based varnish to protect the surface.

This startlingly original mirror frame, which resembles an oval flowerbed full of daffodil blooms, is made from humble egg cartons, yet has a delicacy reminiscent of fine ceramic or plasterwork.

Egg Carton Frame

you will need

tracing paper

pencil

corrugated cardboard

craft knife

cutting mat

rectangular mirror, 3mm/⅛in thick, cut to size

strong glue stick or PVA (white) glue

gummed paper tape, optional

white egg cartons

small scissors

emulsion (latex) paint: white

paintbrush

matt white aerosol (spray) paint

protective face mask

strong adhesive tape

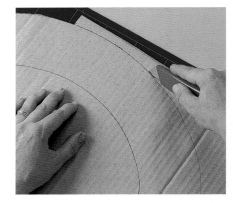

1 Enlarge the frame template from the back of the book, transfer on to a sheet of corrugated cardboard, and cut out two shapes using a craft knife and working on a cutting mat.

2 Cut a smaller oval centre out of one piece and a rectangular shape to fit the mirror from the other. Glue the two together. If you wish, use gummed paper tape to disguise the raw edges.

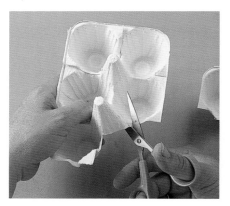

3 Cut out all the cups from the egg cartons, leaving the taller, central dividing sections intact.

4 Cut each cup into five petal shapes. Use the ridges as the petal centres because they look most realistic. You will need at least 50 of them to make daffodils with plenty of petals.

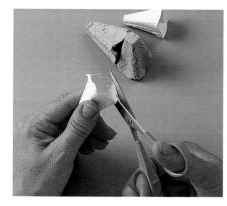

5 Make the daffodil trumpets from the central parts of the cartons, cutting a wavy edge around each one.

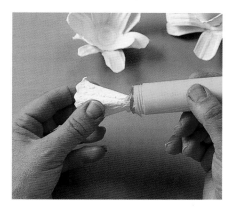

6 Assemble the daffodils using a strong glue stick or PVA (white) glue. Glue two petal sections on top of each other, then add a centre.

7 Once the glue has bonded, the flowers can be moulded into shape by pressing the petals outwards and rounding off the centres.

8 Paint the frame base white and leave it to dry. If you used gummed paper tape to disguise the cardboard edges, this can also be painted white.

9 Glue the daffodils around the frame to cover the base completely. Apply several coats of matt white spray paint, wearing a mask for protection. Secure the mirror in the rebate at the back using strong adhesive tape. Paper over it for a neat finish.

This delicate copper frame is decorated using a simple embossing technique called repoussé. Impressing the back of the foil using a dry ballpoint pen creates an intricate raised design that sparkles in the light.

Repoussé Frame

you will need

0.1mm/¹⁄₂₅₀in copper foil

adhesive tape

protective pad

dry ballpoint pen

ruler

dressmaker's tracing wheel

small, pointed scissors

foam board

double-sided carpet tape or

all-purpose glue

1 Enlarge the template at the back of the book on a photocopier. Tape the copy to a sheet of copper foil. Rest the foil on a protective pad and transfer the design by drawing lightly over the lines with a dry ballpoint pen. Use a ruler for the straight lines. Remove the tracing paper, then press more firmly with the pen over the lightly drawn lines. Use a constant even pressure to make the marks consistent.

2 Use a tracing wheel to outline the outer and inner edges and add the detail to the crown. Use the ballpoint pen to draw the crossed lines between the tracing wheel outlines. Then draw a star in each scallop around the edge by making four crossed lines.

3 Cut around the frame with scissors. Cut out the centre. Cut out a sheet of foam board in the shape of the frame. Mount your picture in the centre of the foam board and attach the metal frame to the foam board, embossed side down, with double-sided carpet tape or all-purpose glue.

Because of its softness, fine-gauge aluminium foil is the perfect material for cladding frames. Coloured and clear glass nuggets combine with the subdued tones of the foil to give this frame a Celtic style.

Celtic Jewelled Frame

you will need
wide, flat frame
ruler
0.1mm/$\frac{1}{250}$in thick aluminium foil
scissors
epoxy resin glue
pencil
thin cardboard
dry ballpoint pen
coloured and clear glass nuggets

1 Remove the glass and backing from the frame. Measure the four sides and cut strips of foil to cover them, making the foil long enough to wrap over and under, to the back. Mould the foil strips around the frame and glue them in place. Cut pieces of foil to cover the corners. Mould these to the contours of the frame and glue in place.

2 Draw a circle on cardboard and cut it out to make a template. Draw around the cardboard on to the foil using a dry ballpoint pen. Determine how many circles will fit around your frame, then cut out the foil circles. Draw a design on to one side of each circle. This is the back.

3 Turn the foil circles over so that the raised side of the embossing is face up. Glue coloured glass nuggets to the centre of half of the foil circles, and clear glass nuggets to the other half. Glue the foil circles evenly around the frame, alternating coloured glass and clear glass centres. Replace the glass and backing in the frame.

Copper against glass gives a bright, fresh look, making it a perfect treatment for this round mirror. Rolls of self-adhesive copper foil can be bought from stained-glass suppliers and it is very easy to apply.

Copper Foil Mirror

you will need

straight-edged self-adhesive copper foil tape, 1cm/½in wide

round mirror, 3mm/⅛in thick

wooden clothes peg (pin)

scalloped self-adhesive copper foil tape, 1cm/½in wide

tracing paper

pencil

scissors

sheet of self-adhesive copper foil

adhesive plate-holder disc

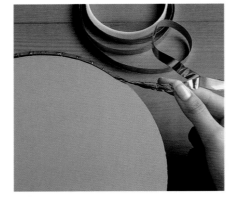

1 Roll a length of straight-edged copper foil tape around the raw edge of the mirror glass, so that equal parts fall on each side.

2 Press down with a wooden clothes peg (pin) on both sides.

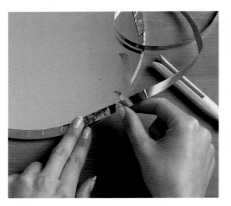

3 Add a second rim of straight-edged copper foil tape to the mirror surface only, covering the edge of your original border. Add a further rim of scalloped copper foil tape, again just overlapping the last border. Press down each layer of tape with the peg.

4 Trace the template at the back of the book, and use this to draw and cut out several leaves from the sheet of self-adhesive copper foil. Cut out several small circles too. Stick the leaves into position on the mirror, and stick the small circles in between them.

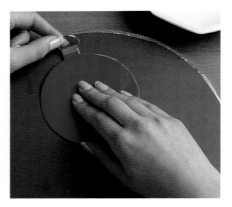

5 To hang the mirror, coat an adhesive plate-holder disc with water, wait until it is tacky, then stick it on to the back of the mirror.

In this striking design, a delicately-marked feather is sandwiched between two sheets of glass which are edged in lead. You may also wish to gild the outer area of glass using the verre eglomisé technique.

Lead Frame

you will need
2 pieces of glass
cloth
methylated spirits (denatured alcohol)
4 wood fillets, 5mm/¼in thick
pencil
craft knife or hacksaw
cutting mat
thick black marker pen
epoxy resin glue
bradawl (awl)
nylon thread
feather or other lightweight object
weight
protective gloves
scissors, optional
self-adhesive lead
plastic smoothing tool
self-adhesive hangers

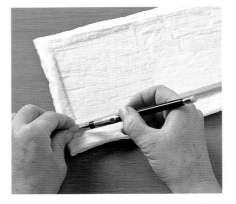

1 Clean the glass thoroughly with a cloth dipped in methylated spirits (denatured alcohol). Measure the wood fillets against the sides of one piece of glass and mark with a pencil where they are to be cut.

2 Once the fillets have been measured and marked, cut along the pencil line with a craft knife on a cutting mat. Alternatively, use a hacksaw with a thin blade.

3 Colour the fillets all over with a thick black marker pen. Using epoxy resin glue, stick the blackened fillets around three sides of one piece of glass, leaving the top section open.

4 Using a bradawl (awl), make a small hole in the remaining fillet and pass a length of nylon thread through it. Secure this. On the other end of the nylon thread, stick the feather with epoxy resin glue.

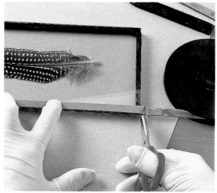

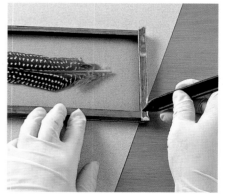

5 Centre the feather in the frame and stick the remaining top fillet to the glass. Place small drops of epoxy resin glue on all four fillets then place the second piece of glass on top. Leave to set for approximately 10–15 minutes, preferably with a weight on top.

6 Wearing protective gloves and using scissors or a craft knife, cut self-adhesive lead strips to the size of the glass edges, just overlapping each edge.

7 Warm the lead strip in the palm of your hand for a few seconds. Remove the backing strip, place the lead strip on the glass edge and apply pressure with a plastic smoothing tool. Trim off the excess. Continue all around the frame. Attach self-adhesive hangers to the back of the frame.

Tin is a soft metal that can be decorated easily using a centre punch or a blunt chisel to create dots and lines. Keep your punched design graphic and uncluttered, as too much fine detail will get lost.

Punched Tin Leaf Frame

you will need

wide, flat wooden frame

thin cardboard

felt-tipped pen

scissors

adhesive tape

sheet of tin

centre punch

hammer

tin snips (shears)

protective gloves (optional)

chisel

ridged paint scraper

copper nails

metal polish and cloth, optional

clear varnish and brush, optional

paper towels and salt water, optional

wax and soft cloth, optional

1 Place the wooden frame on a piece of thin cardboard and draw around the outline with a felt-tipped pen. Add borders at the outside and centre edges to allow for turnings, and cut out the template with scissors. Tape the template on to a sheet of tin. Mark the corners using a centre punch and hammer, and mark the straight lines with a felt-tipped pen.

2 Cut out the shape with tin snips. (You may want to wear protective gloves to protect your hands from the tin's sharp edges.) Using a hammer and chisel, cut through the centre of the frame in a diagonal line, then use tin snips to cut along the remaining sides, to leave you with a cut-out square, a little smaller than the centre of the frame.

3 Place the wooden frame on the tin and use a ridged paint scraper to coax the metal up the sides of the frame.

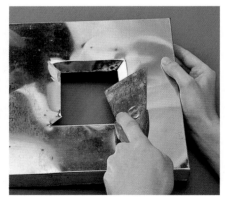

4 Turn the frame over and push down the metal edges in the centre, again using the ridged paint scraper.

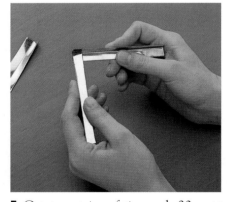

5 Cut two strips of tin, each 20cm × 18mm/8 × ¾in. Snip at the halfway mark and fold at a 90° angle. Nail the strips to the inner edge of the frame, using copper nails.

6 Carefully hammer copper nails along the outer edges of the frame so that the tin is firmly secured in place.

7 Draw a freehand leaf or other design on the tin frame with a felt-tipped pen, remembering to keep the pattern simple and bold for the best effect. Any errors can be easily wiped away from the metal surface.

8 Press the leaf design on to the tin in dots, using a hammer and centre punch. Alternatively, a blunt chisel and hammer can be used to press the design on to the tin in straight lines.

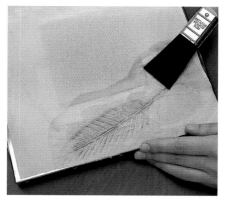

9 There are two ways to finish the frame. Clean the tin with metal polish and a soft cloth, removing any traces of marker pen. To preserve the finish, seal with clear varnish.

10 To rust the frame, cover with a paper towel and dampen with salt water. Keep the paper damp until the frame has rusted (2–7 days). Remove the paper and seal with wax when dry.

This light and airy picture frame is made from thick aluminium wire, which is soft and bends easily to form the filigree frame surround. The pastel ribbon and old-fashioned picture create a Victorian look.

Wire Picture Frame

you will need

round-nosed (snub-nosed) pliers

soft aluminium wire, 3mm/⅛in and 1mm/⅟₂₅in thick

ruler

wire cutters

small-gauge chicken wire

gloves, optional

galvanized wire, 1.5mm/⅟₁₆in thick

permanent marker pen

ribbon

picture

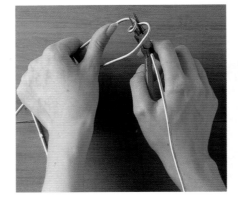

1 Using round-nosed (snub-nosed) pliers, carefully bend the 3mm/⅛ in aluminium wire into a rectangle measuring 15 × 20cm/6 × 8in. At the fourth corner, twist the wire into a heart shape. Do not cut off the wire.

2 Bend the wire into a series of filigree loops to fit along each side of the frame. Form a heart at each corner as you reach it.

3 Leave 1.5cm/½in of excess wire spare at the last corner and cut off.

4 Cut a 15 × 40cm/6 × 16in rectangle of small-gauge chicken wire and fold it in half. Bend the filigree out of the way and use 1mm/⅟₂₅in aluminium wire to bind the chicken wire to the inner rectangle.

5 Bend the filigree back into place and bind it on to the inner rectangle.

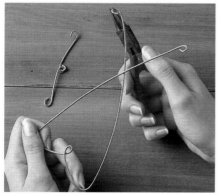

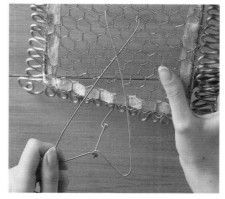

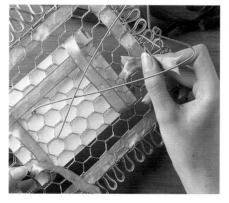

6 To make a support for the frame, cut a 48cm/19in length of galvanized wire. Mark the wire at intervals of 18cm/7in, 6cm/2½in, 6cm/2½in, and 18cm/7in. Bend the wire into a crossed-triangle, forming a loop in the centre and at each end. Cut two short pieces of wire and make a loop at each end. Link the two pieces together and close the loop firmly.

7 Thread the ribbon around the edges of the chicken wire, looping it around each corner so that it lies flat. Attach the support to the frame by opening the loops slightly and then closing them around the chicken wire near the top. Attach one end of the two short linked pieces to the loop in the bottom of the support, and the other end to the base of the frame.

8 Position your picture on the frame and secure it by threading a ribbon through the wire from the back, and looping it around the corners.

This attractive frame incorporates two metal foils, one copper and one brass. The brass pins used to attach the foil to the frame also form a decorative accent in this otherwise simple design.

Metal Foil Frame

you will need

protective gloves
copper foil
scissors or wire cutters
wide, flat wooden frame
dry ballpoint pen
metal ruler
craft knife
self-healing cutting mat
tack hammer
brass escutcheon pins
bradawl (awl)
brass foil
wire (steel) wool
black felt
scissors
fabric glue and brush

1 Cut pieces of copper foil to fit over the frame, allowing for overlaps around the inner rebate and outer edge. Place the frame face down on the foil. Score the foil with a dry ballpoint pen around the inner rebate and outer edge. Remove the frame. Using a metal ruler and craft knife, cut out the corners on the outer edge in line with the score marks. Cut the inner rebate window and mitre the corners.

2 Fold the inner rebate foil around the moulding. Tack it on to the frame with small brass pins – you will need to make the pin holes with a bradawl (awl). Repeat on the outer edge.

3 Hammer the brass foil in place in the same way. Hammer pins at the edges of the brass foil.

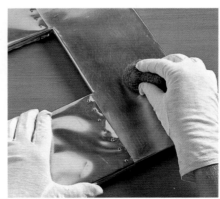

4 Using wire (steel) wool, score the copper foil in small circular motions.

5 Cut a piece of black felt to cover the back of the frame. Cut out the window. Stick in place with fabric glue.

Stylized painting on tinware is part of the popular art of India and Latin America. Fine-gauge tin is stamped with decorative patterns and highlighted with translucent paints. This mirror frame follows the tradition.

Painted Tinware Mirror

you will need

sheet of tin plate, 30 gauge
(0.3mm/¹⁄₈₃in thick)

marker pen

ruler

work shirt and protective
leather gloves

tin snips (shears)

90° and 45° wooden blocks

bench vice

hide hammer

file

graph paper

scissors

saucer

pencil

square mirror tile

masking tape

sheet of chipboard

panel pins (brads)

tack hammer

centre punch

ball hammer

chinagraph pencil

soft cloth

translucent paints

paintbrush

aluminium foil, 36 gauge
(0.1mm/¹⁄₂₅₀in thick)

epoxy resin glue

copper foil, 40 gauge
(0.08mm/¹⁄₃₀₀in thick)

D-ring hanger

1 For the frame, draw a 30cm/12in square on a sheet of tin. Draw a 1cm/½in border inside the square. Draw diagonal lines across the corners of the inner square. Wearing protective clothes, cut out the 30cm/12in square with tin snips (shears). Cut along the diagonal lines at the corners.

2 Firmly clamp the 90° block of wood in a bench vice. Place the mirror frame on the wooden block with the ruled edge of the tin resting on the edge of the block. Using a hide hammer, tap along the edge of the tin to turn it over to an angle of 90°.

3 Turn the frame over. Hold the 45° block of wood inside the turned edge and hammer the edge over. Remove the block and hammer the edge completely flat. Finish the remaining three edges of the frame in the same way. Carefully file the corners of the mirror frame to remove any sharp edges.

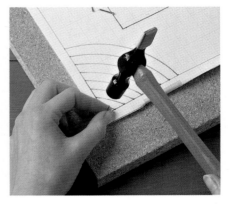

4 Cut a piece of graph paper the same size as the frame. Using a saucer as a template, draw the corner lines on to the paper. Draw in the central square, slightly larger than the mirror tile. Tape the pattern to the back of the frame. Secure the frame to a piece of chipboard with panel pins (brads).

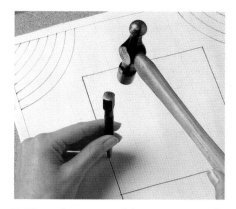

5 Place the point of the centre punch on a drawn line of the inside square and tap it with the ball hammer to make an indentation. Move the punch 3mm/⅛in along the line and tap it to make the next mark. Continue along all the lines.

6 Unpin the frame from the board and remove the pattern. Using a chinagraph pencil, draw a square halfway along each edge between the corner decorations. Draw a heart in each square. Pin the frame to the board again and punch an outline around each square and heart.

7 Randomly punch the border between the heart and the square to make a densely pitted surface. Remove the frame from the board. Wipe over the surface with a soft cloth to remove any grease. Paint the embossed areas of the frame with translucent paints. Leave to dry.

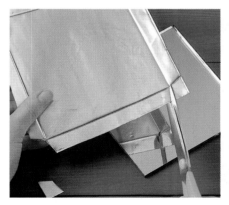

8 Place the mirror tile on aluminium foil and draw around it. Draw a 1.5cm/⅝in border around the outline. Cut out the foil, snipping the corners at right angles. Glue the tile to the centre of the foil. Glue the edges of the foil over the tile. Cut four small squares of copper foil and glue one square in each corner of the tile.

9 Glue the mirror to the centre of the frame. Glue the hanger to the back of the frame. Allow the glue to dry thoroughly before hanging up the mirror.

This imposing little frame is made from nothing more substantial than cardboard, galvanized wire and some metallic paint, yet it looks weighty and solid, and even has its own wire stand.

Zigzag Wire Frame

1 Trace the template at the back of the book. Cut four lengths of 2mm/¹⁄₁₂in wire each 70cm/28in and, using long-nosed pliers, bend each length to match the spiral zigzag shapes along one side of the frame.

2 Cut ten lengths of 2mm/¹⁄₁₂in wire each 30cm/12in and curl each one into a tight S-shape with the pliers.

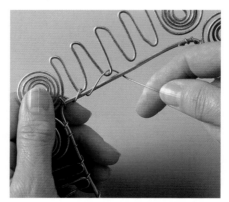

4 Using 1mm/¹⁄₂₅in wire, bind the four side sections to the central frame.

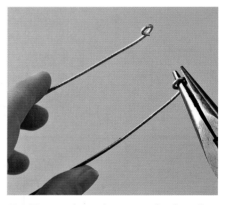

5 To make the stand, bend a 30cm/12in length of 2mm/¹⁄₁₂in wire into a narrow U-shape, then curl each end into a tight loop.

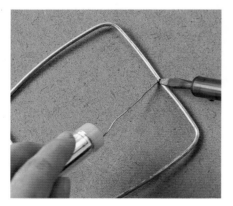

3 Cut a 40cm/16in length of 3mm/¹⁄₈in wire and bend it into a square to form the centre of the picture frame. Arrange the ends in the middle of one side. Solder the ends together.

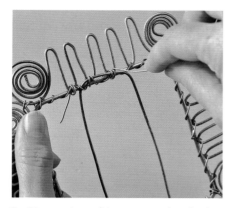

6 Using 1mm/½⁵in wire, bind the stand centrally to the back of the top of the frame.

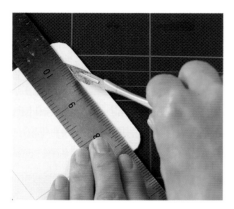

7 Cut two pieces of cardboard to fit the frame, using a craft knife and metal ruler and working on a cutting mat. Cut a window out of the front and a slightly larger window from the back section. Reserve the central part of the back. Stick the frames together using double-sided tape.

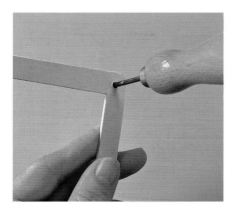

8 Using a bradawl (awl), pierce a small hole in each corner of the picture holder. Paint the front silver.

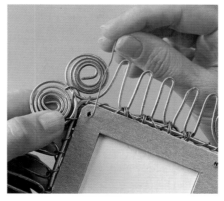

9 Bind the picture holder to the frame at each corner using short lengths of fine wire.

10 Use epoxy resin glue to stick the small S-shapes around the frame. Insert the picture and the cardboard backing board.

Fabric, Beads and Flowers

Fabric, beads and flowers can all be used to embellish a plain frame, to add texture, charm and delicacy. You don't need to be a skilled stitcher to use felt, or an expert gardener to utilize dried and silk flowers, but decorative stitching can add another dimension to a frame, and a garden full of flowers gives you greater choice for drying. What is more important, however, is a feel for the decorative potential of these materials.

Colour and Texture

Fabric, beads and flowers offer a multitude of ways of decorating a frame. Use them singly or combine them to create a heady mix of colour and texture. Unless you are decorating a mirror frame, stick to one or two colours so as not to overpower the central image, or you could echo the theme of the picture in your decoration.

Real flowers and leaves can be used in all sorts of ways to decorate a frame. Use chunky twigs and raffia to create a rustic three-dimensional frame, or combine flowers with fabric for a really decorative project. Try making a circlet of dried herb leaves,

wired or glued together, or create a collage of dried flowerheads in bright summery colours. If real flower colours seem too muted, you can create a splash of colour with massed silk flowers, or even cut simple flower shapes out of brightly coloured plastic.

Felt is a wonderful material for use in frame decoration. Available in a variety of bold colours, it can be cut without fraying, and can be glued or stitched, making it ideal for not-so-nimble fingers.

Try cutting out stylized felt shapes and stitching them together to create an entire frame, or make a patchwork appliqué of felt shapes on a fabric background. Painted silk is another lovely fabric to use, and there is a huge range of silk paints available; stylized patterns or motifs are the easiest to paint, but practise first on a spare piece of fabric.

Beads are available in a range of colours and sizes, making them perfect for use in frame decoration. Together with sequins, they can be used for

sparkly decoration in their own right, or to embellish fabric, flowers or paint. Sprinkle them over the frame, stitch them in place with sewing thread, or

thread them on wire for three-dimensional motifs.

For those seeking something more challenging, this chapter also includes a project for a lovely padded silk frame, and for making a hooked rag design, for which any fabric can be used. Search through your scrap bag for enticing pieces of velvet and silk that you can recycle to make glamorous frames for precious pictures.

Any kind of fabric can be used to cover a frame. As only a small amount is needed for a moderate sized frame, you may want to splash out on the most luxurious silks and velvets to enhance a room scheme.

Materials and Equipment

Embroidery hoop
Fabric is placed in the hoop to keep it taut for hand or machine embroidery or beadwork.

Embroidery thread (floss)
Stranded embroidery thread is available in hundreds of shades, as well as metallics. Use all the strands together for bold stitching, or separate them for finer effects.

Felt
Available from craft suppliers in small squares and in a wide range of brilliant colours, felt does not fray and can be stitched or glued.

Flower press
A large number of flowers, leaves and petals can be pressed at the same time in a flower press. Pressure is exerted by tightening a screw at each corner. A heavy book can also be used, but it should not be a precious volume as the flowers will exude moisture.

Artificial flowers
Silk flowers of many kinds are available from milliners and craft suppliers. Crepe paper flowers could also be used to decorate frames.

Beads
Use tiny rocaille and bugle beads like glitter, sprinkled on to a glued surface. Stitch or glue larger beads on to frames individually. Small beads can also be threaded on to fine wire to create three-dimensional motifs.

Blotting paper
Used for pressing flowers and petals, to absorb moisture. Place sheets in a heavy book with a weight on top, or insert sheets in a flower press.

Craft knife
Used for reducing the bulk of large flowers for pressing.

Dried flowers
Buy commercially dried flowers from florists or dry your own.

Fusible bonding web
This is used to bond fabrics together in appliqué work. It is supplied on backing paper, which makes it easy to draw and cut out shapes.

Glue
Use rubber-solution (latex) fabric glue or carpet adhesive for attaching fabric

covers to frames. Use PVA (white glue) to paint shapes on which to sprinkle small beads or sequins.

Glue gun

This electrically heated gun melts various types of glue supplied in stick form. It gives an instant bond when working with fabric and dried or artificial flowers.

Hessian (burlap)

This strong woven fabric is used as the backing material for ragwork.

Interfacing

Used to reinforce fabrics. Iron-on interfacing is a non-woven material which can be bonded to the wrong side of the fabric.

Iron

Used to set silk paints and iron on fusible bonding web for appliqué. It can also be used to press flowers between sheets of blotting paper.

Metallic gutta

Used to define designs on silk before painting, to prevent the paints bleeding into one another. It is applied using a special applicator which allows fine details to be defined.

Plastic

For a fun frame treatment, cut plastic flower shapes out of plastic bottles and cartons in bright colours.

Raffia

Use undyed raffia to bind twigs, seedheads and other natural materials to decorate frames.

Ribbon

Satin ribbon can be used to trim frames; stronger ribbons such as petersham or grosgrain can be woven together to cover the whole frame. Small ribbon roses make a pretty decoration for silk-covered frames.

Rug hook

This simple hook on a wooden handle is used to hook strips of rag through hessian (burlap) in ragwork. It is available from craft suppliers.

Scissors

Reserve a pair of sharp scissors exclusively for cutting fabrics, as paper and other materials will quickly blunt their edges. Use large scissors for cutting fabric and small, sharp pointed scissors for embroidery threads.

Sequins

These are available in numerous shapes, sizes and colours, separately or sewn into strings. Stitch or glue them to the frame.

Sewing machine

For joining fabrics and for machine embroidery.

Silk paints

These fabric paints can be used to create delicate washes of colour as well as more vibrant effects. Stretch the silk on a wooden frame to hold it taut. The colours can be set using an iron.

Silk pins

These three-pronged pins are used to secure silk stretched over a frame without ripping the fabric.

Staple gun

Used to attach fabric quickly and easily to a wooden frame.

Twigs and sticks

Collect natural objects from the garden or when out walking. Bundles of willow or hazel sticks of equal size can be bought from craft suppliers or garden centres.

Twine

Jute and sisal twine of various thicknesses make natural looking bindings or hangers for frames, or can be coiled into decorations.

Vanishing fabric marker pen

This dressmaker's aid is useful for marking the right side of fabrics when drawing complex designs, as the marks fade away once the work is completed.

Wadding (batting)

Used to back fabrics when making padded frames.

Pressing flowers

Always pick flowers when they are fully open and gather flowers and leaves for pressing on a dry sunny day as any additional moisture in the plant material will lengthen the pressing process.

Preparing

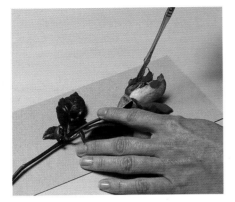

1 Using a craft knife, cut any very bulky flowerheads, such as roses, in half. Then press the flowers.

2 Reduce the height of a thick calyx by snipping close to the petals with small scissors. Be careful not to snip too closely or the petals may fall out.

3 Pare down thick stems using a craft knife. To remove excess moisture from a fleshy stem, place it between the layers of a folded piece of paper towel and squeeze with your fingers.

Pressing

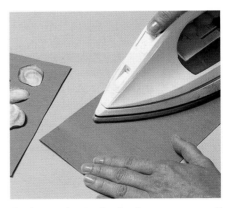

1 The simplest method of pressing flowers is to use a large book. Lay the petals or leaves face down on a folded piece of blotting paper and place between the pages of the book. Put a weight on top, and leave in a warm, dry place for about 6 weeks.

2 To press individual petals, lay them out on a folded piece of blotting paper and press between the pages of a book, as in step 1.

3 A quick method of pressing small flowers, leaves or petals is to iron them. Place them inside a folded piece of blotting paper, and iron using a moderate setting.

Rug hooking

In ragwork, strips of material are hooked through a hessian (burlap) backing cloth. They can be left as a loop pile surface, or sheared with scissors to create a cut pile surface. An effective use of hooking is to combine cut and loop pile within one piece.

Backing

1 Place one hand underneath the frame, and loop a strip of fabric between your thumb and forefinger. With your other hand above the frame, push the hook through the hessian (burlap). Feed the fabric loop on to the hook. (The picture shows the underside of the frame.)

2 Pull the hook back up through the hessian, bringing the end of the strip of fabric through to the top.

Using the finished ragwork as a template, cut out a slightly larger piece of felt. Pin round the edge to attach it in position on the back of the work. Take a needle and matching thread, and slip stitch round the edge, tucking under the excess fabric as you sew.

3 Leave one or two warp threads of hessian to keep the loops close together. Push the hook back through the hessian and feed the fabric loop on to the hook, as before. Pull the hook back up through the hessian to make a loop, approximately 1cm/½in high. Continue. Bring the ends of fabric through to the top, and trim to the same height as the loops.

4 To create a cut pile surface, repeat steps 1–3 but hook the loops to a height of approximately 2cm/¾in. Shear across the top of the loops with a large pair of scissors.

Dried poppy seedheads, a selection of twigs and a little paint are all that are needed to decorate these wooden frames. Arrange the materials until you are happy with the designs, then glue them in position.

Poppy Seedhead Frames

you will need

For each frame:

wooden frame, prepared and sanded

multi-purpose glue and brush

brown paper

craft knife

Poppies and Twigs Frame

emulsion (latex) paint

PVA (white) glue

soft cloth

twigs

dried poppy seedheads

Sticks Frame

lichen-covered twigs

multi-purpose glue

Poppies Frame

brown paper tape

dried poppy seedheads

watercolour paint: brown

fine artist's paintbrush

1 To make the Poppies and Twigs Frame (pictured bottom left in the photograph), and the Sticks Frame (pictured bottom right), glue torn strips of brown paper around the front edges of a wooden frame.

2 For the Poppies and Twigs Frame, dilute the paint and add 5ml/1 tsp glue. Paint a thin colourwash over the frame using the paint and glue mixture. Before it dries, wipe it off with a soft cloth to leave a very thin coat.

3 To decorate the Poppies and Twigs Frame, select twigs and seedheads and cut them to size. Cut through the seedheads with a craft knife.

4 Plan your design first, then use glue to stick each piece in position.

5 To make the Sticks Frame, glue lichen-covered twigs around the prepared frame. Leave overnight to dry.

6 To make the Poppies Frame (pictured at the top), cover the back and front of the wooden frame with strips of brown paper tape.

7 Glue rough strips of torn brown paper on to the frame.

8 Add pattern and interest to the brown paper with watercolour paint brushed on in fine cross-hatched lines.

9 Cut off the top of the dried poppy heads with a craft knife and glue them on to the frame.

Natural linen and linen tape tone beautifully with the pressed flowers and leaves, and the colourwashed wooden frame, in this attractive design. Use the noticeboard for messages, postcards and reminders.

Country-style Noticeboard

you will need

wooden frame, prepared and sanded

paintbrush

emulsion (latex) paint: off-white

pressed flowers, such as daisies and small white chrysanthemums

pressed leaves, such as senecio and artemisia

tape measure

PVA (white) glue

fine artist's brush

matt acrylic spray varnish

protective face mask

medium density fibreboard (MDF)

saw

natural linen

scissors

staple gun

soft pencil

linen dressmaking tape

decorative upholstery nails

hammer

picture wire, optional

1 Paint the picture frame lightly with off-white emulsion (latex) paint so that the texture of the wood shows through. Leave to dry.

2 Plan the arrangement of the flowers and leaves on the frame. Start in the centre of one short side and work outwards, using a tape measure if necessary. Apply a little PVA (white) glue to the back of each flower or leaf and stick in place.

3 Spray the frame with matt acrylic varnish to seal the surface. Apply two coats if necessary, but take care not to flatten the flowers.

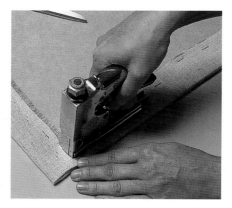

4 Wearing a protective face mask, cut a piece of medium density fibreboard (MDF) to fit inside the frame. Cover with linen, securing the fabric at the back with a staple gun.

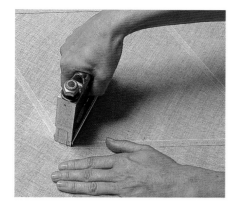

5 On the right side, mark out a large diamond in the centre, using a soft pencil. Cut four lengths of linen tape to fit and lay in place, stapling them together at the corners.

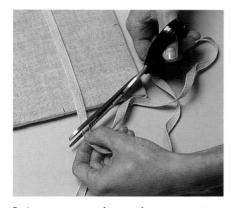

6 Arrange more lines of tape, weaving them over and under in a diamond pattern. Trim the tape ends and staple to the back of the board.

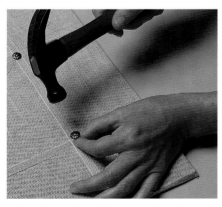

7 On the right side, secure the lines of tape with upholstery nails spaced at regular intervals. Fit the decorated board into the frame. Attach picture wire at the top for hanging, if required.

This frame has a warm, autumnal feel about it, and would make a delightful souvenir of a woodland walk. When collecting the leaves, look for those with unusual colours and shapes.

Pressed-leaf Frame

✿✿

you will need

selection of leaves in various colours

paper towels

flower press or heavy book

PVA (white) glue and brush

wooden frame, prepared and sanded

acrylic varnish and brush

acrylic crackle glaze

oil paint: raw umber

soft cloth

1 To press leaves, place between layers of paper towels between the pages of a heavy book. Leave for a week.

2 Glue the leaves on to the frame, coating them one at a time with a thin layer of glue and waiting for it to get tacky before sticking the leaf down. Begin by arranging a row of overlapping leaves around the outer edge of the frame. Make a second round, using a different leaf. Select four larger leaves for the corners. Fill in any gaps.

3 Paint a thin layer of varnish over the whole surface and allow to dry. Paint the frame with crackle glaze, following the manufacturer's instructions. Rub a small amount of raw umber oil paint into the cracks in the glaze with a soft cloth, to emphasize the antique effect.

This green and twiggy frame will give your room a log cabin touch. A group of frames could be used to display a variety of natural objects. Look for a discarded fruit packing crate at a local street market.

Rustic Picture Frame

❁ ❁

you will need
plywood packing crate
craft knife
cutting mat
metal ruler
heavy-duty stapler
paper
large scissors
PVA (white) glue and glue brush
artificial grass
spoon
assorted twigs and sticks
wood glue
raffia

1 Dismantle the packing crate. Using a craft knife and metal ruler, cut three of the planks from the crate to the same size. These will sit side by side to form the background for the picture. Cut two small battens, a little shorter than the width of the three planks. Staple them across the three planks, at the top and bottom.

2 Mask off the required picture area with paper. Coat the frame around it with glue, then sprinkle with artificial grass. Shake off the excess. Cut twigs 11.5cm/4½in long. Glue in place in a diamond pattern, using wood glue.

3 Cut four thicker sticks to make a border around the outer frame, and four to make a border around the picture area. Tie together with raffia. Glue in place using wood glue. Leave to dry. Insert your chosen image.

There is something very satisfying about producing attractive items from everyday materials. All you need to make this simple frame are jute twine and a piece of cardboard.

Twine Picture Frame

you will need
sturdy cardboard
pencil
set square
ruler
craft knife
cutting mat
jute twine
scissors
high-tack PVA (white) glue
glue spreader

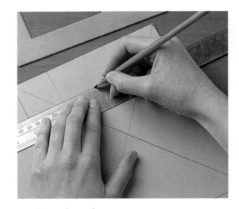

1 Decide what size you want your frame to be; draw the dimensions on to cardboard using a set square and ruler. To find the centre, draw diagonal lines from corner to corner. Then draw the window for the front of the picture frame.

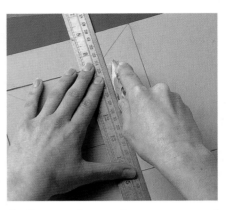

2 Cut out the window using a craft knife and working on a cutting mat. Do not attempt to cut through the entire thickness of the board at once: instead make several shallow cuts.

3 Cut a length of jute twine. Apply glue to a short section of one side of the frame and wrap it with the twine. Wrap the string closely together for an even finish.

4 At the end of the first piece of twine, tie on a new length of twine at the back with a knot. Apply more glue as you work around the frame.

5 When you reach a corner, turn the frame 90° and continue along the next side of the frame, leaving the corner unwrapped. Cover all four sides.

6 Wrap twine diagonally across each corner. Cover one half of the corner and then the other. Cut off any loose ends of the twine and glue them down.

7 Cut a piece of sturdy cardboard slightly smaller than the wrapped frame and glue it on to the back.

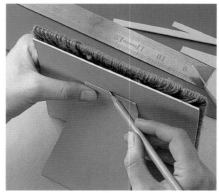

8 Cut a stand from sturdy cardboard. Mark its position on the back of the frame and glue in place.

This frame shows how ordinary material can be used decoratively. Sisal string is glued into loops and spirals, allowed to dry, then stuck in place. Leave the string in its natural state or finish it with a coat of paint.

String Spirals Frame

you will need

paper

pencil

pair of compasses

scissors

corrugated cardboard

pen

PVA (white) glue and brush

sisal string

craft knife

emulsion (latex) paint: matt white

paintbrush

1 Draw 5cm/2in diameter circles on paper using a pair of compasses and cut out to use as templates. Draw around the circles on the corrugated cardboard to make a frame shape.

2 Starting in the middle of the circles and working outwards, glue on sisal string in spirals. Fill in each of the circles in this way.

3 At the corners of the frame, fill in the spaces with smaller spirals of string.

4 When the glue is completely dry, cut around the edge of the frame with a craft knife.

5 Tidy the cut edges of the corrugated cardboard by gluing two lengths of sisal string over them.

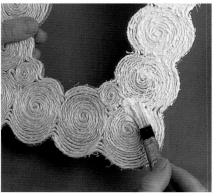

6 Paint the front of the frame with matt white emulsion (latex) paint.

7 Make a cardboard back and stand for the frame. Paint them white and allow to dry. Glue the stand in place.

These sparkly picture frames are easy to make. Treat small coloured rocaille and bugle beads like glitter and simply pour them generously on to the glued surface of the frames.

Bead-encrusted Frames

you will need

wooden frames, prepared and sanded

emulsion (latex) or acrylic paint

paintbrushes

palette or plate

PVA (white) glue and brush

small glass rocaille beads in a variety of colours

large sheet of paper

glitter

bugle beads in a variety of colours

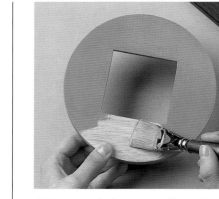

1 Paint each frame in a flat colour and allow to dry. Add another coat if necessary to ensure the bare wood is completely covered.

2 Paint a heart in one corner of a square frame, using glue. Sprinkle rocaille beads over the glue. After the beads have settled for a minute, lightly tap the frame to remove any loose ones. Repeat with different colour beads on each corner. Leave to dry.

3 Paint the rest of the frame with glue. With the frame on a large sheet of paper, sprinkle on the glitter. Tap off the excess.

4 Decorate a round frame using bugle beads in various shades of the same colour. Apply glue around the centre of the frame and sprinkle on the beads.

5 Gradually work out to the edge of the frame, applying darker or lighter beads to produce a shaded effect.

This delicate frame encrusted with sequins and beads has a nostalgic character that would suit a special family photograph. Some skill or practice with a needle is required for this project.

Sequins and Beads

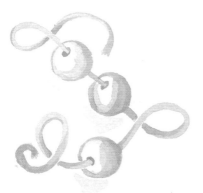

you will need

pencil

metal ruler

mount (mat) board

cutting mat

craft knife

white calico

scissors

needle

matching sewing thread

satin-backed velvet ribbon, 6cm/2½ in wide

green ribbon, 8mm/⅜ in wide

small gold glass beads

translucent sequins

clear crystals

1 Draw the shape of the frame on to mount (mat) board. The frame should be 4cm/1½ in wide. Working on a cutting mat, cut out the frame, using a metal ruler and craft knife.

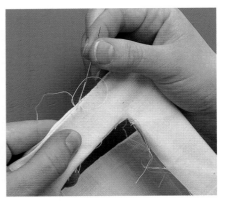

2 Cover the back and front of the frame with white calico, oversewing the edges and turning under the raw edges as you go.

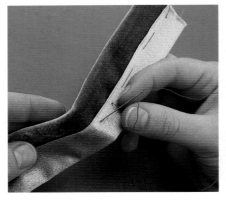

3 Measure around the four sides of the frame and cut a piece of satin-backed ribbon slightly longer than this measurement. Fold the ribbon so it is the same width as the sides of the frame, and baste down the satin edge.

4 Using the covered frame as a guide, fold and mitre the corners of the ribbon, tucking under the raw ends.

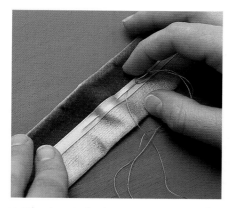

5 Neatly stitch the narrow green ribbon over the seam, using a matching thread colour.

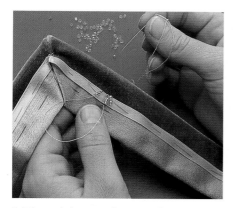

6 Thread four or five small gold glass beads on to a needle and stitch down vertically over the green ribbon. Keeping the beading dense, continue to stitch the beads in place so that the green ribbon is barely visible. Neatly stitch the ribbon frame to the calico-covered frame.

7 Stitch a random selection of translucent sequins and glass beads over the outside edge of the frame.

8 Sew random clear crystals and small glass beads on to the inside edge of the frame.

9 Stitch ribbon to the back of the frame to hold a picture. Leave the top edge unstitched.

Threaded on fine wire, small beads can be turned into enchanting flowers to decorate a plain picture frame. The colours of the translucent glass beads mimic the delicate hues found in real flower petals.

Flowered Frame

❀❀❀
you will need

tape measure

wire cutters

beading wire, 0.4mm and 0.2mm

round-nosed (snub-nosed)
jewellery pliers

small glass beads: pink, yellow
and white

floss thread

wooden frame, prepared and sanded

drill and small drill bit

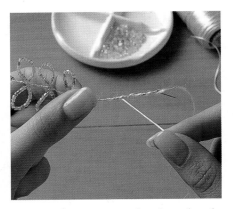

1 To make the leaves, cut 22cm/8¾in of 0.4mm wire. Bend a small hook in one end with pliers to stop the beads falling off. Mix up a few pink beads with the yellow. Bend the wire in half to find the centre point. Thread on 18 beads, push up to the centre point, then bend the wire over to form a beaded loop. Twist the working wire around the stem to secure the beads.

2 Thread on 18 more beads and make another loop. Wrap the working wire around the stem another time and make another loop at the same level. Make two more pairs of loops along the length of the stem. Twist the wire around the stem to secure the beads. Cover the twisted stem by wrapping it with floss thread.

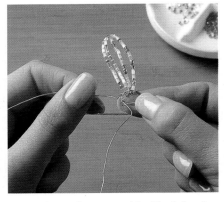

3 Cut 40cm/16in of wire to make a small flower, and 50cm/20in for a large flower. Measure 10cm/4in from one end. Wind the next length of wire twice around your finger to form a loop. The loop is the frame for the beaded flower. Twist the wire to secure the loop.

4 On the next length of wire, pick up 24 pink and white beads for a small flower and 30 for a large one. Push the beads up to the loop framework. Bend the beaded wire back down to the loop frame and twist to secure it.

5 To form the second half of the first petal, thread on some more beads. Twist the wire around the top of the petal and at a right angle to it. Secure the beads on the petal in the same way.

6 Twist the wire around the frame. Make four more petals positioned evenly around the frame.

7 To make the flower centre, thread on 12 yellow beads and twist the wire into a half spiral. Push the working wire through the loop frame and twist it around the stem. The flower centre will stand proud of the frame, and the frame should be covered in beads.

8 Place the flowers and leaves around the frame. When you are happy with the arrangement, mark their positions and drill holes in the frame.

9 Push the wire stems of the beaded flowers and leaves through the holes in the frame and twist them into a knot on the wrong side of the frame.

10 Trim the wire ends. Using the thinner wire, secure the knots on the wrong side of the frame.

A lightweight silk is best for this project, which uses salt to create a soft, watery effect. The silk needs to be damp for the salt grains to take effect, so alternate between painting and adding salt.

Padded Silk Picture Frame

you will need

silk pins

lightweight, plain-weave silk, pre-washed

wooden silk-painting frame

iron-fix (set) silk paints

fine artist's paintbrushes

teaspoon

fine table salt

ruler

pencil

graph paper

craft knife

cutting mat

PVA (white) glue and glue brush

mount (mat) board

25cm/10in square wadding (batting)

dressmaker's scissors

adhesive tape

dressmaker's pins

needle

matching sewing thread

ribbon rose decorations, optional

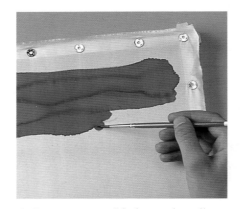

1 Pin a piece of lightweight silk, at least 30cm/12in square, to a silk-painting frame. Using iron-fix (set) silk paints, paint a few stripes of alternate colours on the silk, making the stripes at least 2.5cm/1in wide.

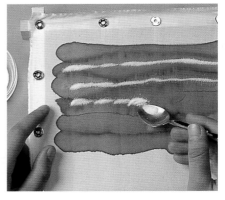

2 While the silk is still damp with the dye, spoon lines of salt grains along the stripes. Continue alternating painting and adding lines of salt grains until the whole surface is covered. Leave the silk to dry. Brush off the salt and iron-fix (set) the dyes according to the manufacturer's instructions.

3 Draw a 20cm/8in square on graph paper and cut out. Draw a 10cm/4in square centrally in it and cut it out. Glue the template to the mount (mat) board and cut out the shape.

4 Centre the frame over a square of wadding (batting). Trim off the corners, then fold and stick the surplus wadding down with adhesive tape. Cut a cross in the centre of the wadding, trim it to 2cm/¾in. Clip into the corners, then fold it to the back of the frame and stick it down.

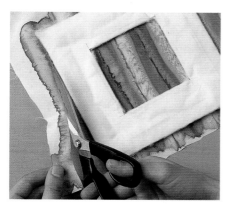

5 Pin the silk to the padded frame, with the wrong side of the silk against the wadding. Trim the excess silk around the frame to 3cm/1¼in. Then cut a cross in the silk inside the frame and trim to 3cm/1¼in all round.

6 Wrap the silk edges over the frame and lace them together with long stitches. Do not pull the silk too tightly and distort the shape.

7 Mitre the corners, fold the flaps over and stitch in place at the back. Sew a small ribbon rose to each inside corner of the frame, if desired.

8 Cut a 20cm/8in square of mount board to make the backing for the frame. Cut a tall, right-angled triangle from the mount board, score along the longest side 1cm/½in from the edge and bend it over to make a stand. Trim the bottom edge and check the board will stand properly.

9 Glue the stand to the backing, starting from the bottom edge. Attach the backing to the frame by gluing along three sides, leaving one side free so that a picture can be slipped inside.

This picture frame has been covered with heavy fabric, then decorated using a square stencil and embellished with gold leaf – an adaptation of the traditional use of gilding on frames.

Painted Fabric Picture Frame

you will need
heavy cardboard
ruler
set square (T-square)
cutting mat
craft knife
scissors
canvas, linen or heavy silk
spray adhesive
vanishing fabric marker pen
double-sided tape
needle
matching sewing thread
masking tape
stencil card (card stock)
fabric paint: deep red
stencil brush
gold size
gold leaf
soft brush
PVA (white) glue and glue brush
clear varnish or lacquer
paintbrush

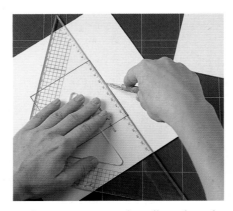

1 Cut two pieces of cardboard to the size required for the frame. Cut a central window in one piece of cardboard. The frame illustrated has a total area of 21cm/8½in square, with a central window of 9cm/3½in square.

2 Cut a piece of canvas, linen or heavy silk 2cm/¾in larger all round than the frame. Apply spray adhesive to the frame and centre it on the fabric, wrong side up. Rub your hand over the cardboard to form a secure bond.

3 Using a vanishing fabric marker pen draw two diagonals across the window. Measure and cut out a 5cm/2in square in the centre of the frame. Clip into the corners.

4 Apply strips of double-sided tape all around the reverse edges of the frame. Pull the extra fabric back and stick it to the tape. Mitre each corner and hand-sew in place.

5 To keep the back of the frame neat, place masking tape over the raw edges of the fabric.

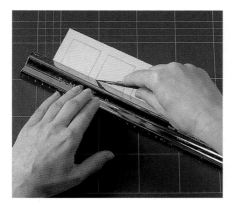

6 Using a craft knife, cut a piece of stencil card (card stock) to a rectangle the same size as one side of the frame, corner to corner (21 × 6cm/8½ × 2½in for the frame illustrated). Mark out equally-spaced squares along the length (4cm/1½in squares with a 1cm/½in division), and cut out.

7 Using masking tape, stick the stencil to one side of the front of the frame. Align the edges. Fill in the squares with deep red fabric paint using a stencil brush and allow to dry. Remove the stencil and fix it to the next side, matching the corner squares, and continue until all four sides have been coloured.

8 Following the manufacturer's instructions, apply a gold leaf square inside the stencilled one. Leave for about 2 hours to set, then remove the loose pieces of gold leaf and buff up the gilding.

9 To make the frame stand, using heavy cardboard and a craft knife, cut out a right-angled triangle of the same height as the frame and 10cm/4in wide. Score along the longest side 1cm/½in from the edge and use PVA (white) glue to stick it to the backing board cut out in step 1.

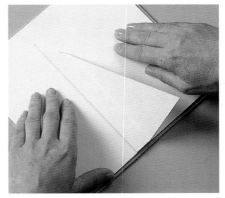

10 Apply glue to the reverse of the backing board on three sides and stick it to the frame. The top is left open to slide in a picture. To protect the gold leaf and to prevent dust from collecting on the fabric, paint the front of the frame with clear varnish or lacquer.

Ribbons are a quick method of adding instant style to a plain picture frame. This design is easy to apply: the ribbons are just woven together at the corners and stapled in place.

Ribbonwork Frame

you will need

medium density fibreboard (MDF),
330 x 250 x 2mm/13 x 10 x ⅛in

pencil

metal ruler

drill and protective face mask

craft knife

wood strip, 106 x 2.5 x 1.25cm/
42 x 1 x ½in

saw

sandpaper (glasspaper)

wood glue and glue spreader

staple gun

hammer

primer: white

paintbrush

navy and white striped ribbon,
5.5m x 15mm/6yd x ⅝in

scissors

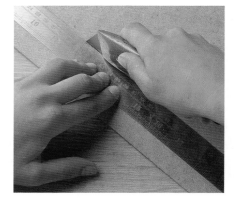

1 To mark out the window area of the frame on the medium density fibreboard (MDF), draw a border 4.75cm/1⅞in from the edges. Drill a small hole at each corner in the window area of the frame, then cut out the window between the holes using a metal ruler and craft knife. Wear a protective face mask when working with MDF. Make several shallow cuts rather than one deep one.

2 Saw the wood strip into two pieces, 33cm/13in long and two pieces 20cm/8in long. Sand the ends and glue them on top of the frame, aligning raw edges. This wood forms the rebate. Staple each joint. Turn the frame over to the right side and staple the MDF to the wood. Hammer the staples flush. Sand any rough edges and apply two coats of white primer. Allow to dry.

3 Cut the ribbon into six 38cm/15in lengths and six 30cm/12in lengths. Spread glue over the front of the frame. Arrange the ribbons on the frame and weave the corners.

4 Lift the frame on to its side. Fold the ribbon ends over the edge and staple down. Once one end of each ribbon is stapled, pull the other end tightly before stapling. Trim the ribbon ends.

5 Glue the remaining ribbon around the edge of the frame with the join at the base. Staple a small piece of ribbon over the join to conceal it.

Felt is a great material because it does not fray when cut and it can be either sewn or glued in place. It is available in vivid colours, so it is ideal for a bright, modern interior.

Felt Collage Frame

you will need

scissors

medium density fibreboard (MDF)

marker pen

protective face mask

jigsaw

emulsion (latex) paint

paintbrush

felt sheets in selection of colours

ballpoint pen

fabric glue and brush

1 On a photocopier enlarge the template provided at the back of the book. Cut out the template, place it on the medium density fibreboard (MDF) and draw around it. Wearing a protective face mask, cut out the frame with a jigsaw. Apply two coats of paint to the frame and leave it to dry.

2 Place the frame on a sheet of felt and draw round the edge with a pen.

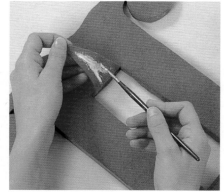

3 Cut out the felt and glue it to the front of the frame. Glue the centre flaps back over the rebate on to the back of the frame.

4 Cut out a zigzag border and stick it to the inner edge. Glue strips of felt around the rebate. Cut out felt decorations and stick them to the frame.

This frame can be used to enhance a small handpainted picture, embroidery or tapestry. Spend some time experimenting with colours, choosing them carefully to complement the subject they will frame.

Stitched Felt Frame

you will need

pencil

cardboard

scissors

vanishing fabric marker pen

interfacing, 10 × 10.5cm/4 × 4¼in

felt, 10 × 10.5cm/4 × 4¼in

fabric glue and glue brush

sewing machine with darning foot

metallic thread

sewing threads

needle

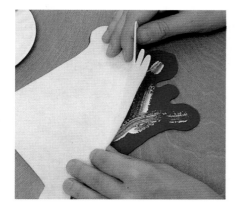

1 Draw and cut out the template provided for the frame. Using a vanishing fabric marker pen, trace around the template on to interfacing and a piece of felt. Cut out the fabric frame and glue the two pieces together.

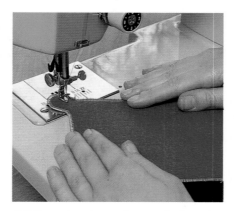

2 When the glue is dry, stitch the edge of the fabric together with metallic thread using fine satin stitch. Change the sewing machine foot to a darning foot. Complete the decoration inside the edge of the frame with filigree.

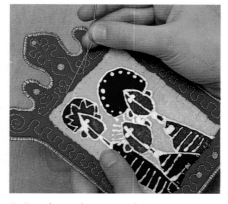

3 Stitch or glue your chosen image on to the middle of the frame.

Felt is easy to use because it has plenty of body and does not fray. Combine two or three different-coloured felts to make a mirror frame in a fun flowery design to hang on the wall.

Fun Felt Frame

❀❀

you will need

iron

fusible bonding web

felt squares, one each in orange and lime, and two in lilac

felt-tipped pen

sharp scissors

small circular mirror

craft knife

needle

matching embroidery threads (floss)

1 Iron the fusible bonding web to the orange, lime and one lilac felt square. On the lilac piece draw a flower outline on the backing paper using the template provided. Draw smaller flowers on the orange and lime squares.

2 Cut out the three felt flower shapes with sharp scissors. Remove the backing paper from the lilac flower and bond it to the other lilac square. Cut around the outline to make a double layer flower.

3 Peel the backing paper off the lime flower and centre it on the lilac one. Fuse the lime flower in place. On the back of the orange flower draw a small circle in the centre, slightly smaller than the mirror, and cut it out.

4 Using a craft knife, make a small cut across the centre of the lime green felt flower, through all three layers of felt. Fuse the orange flower on top of the lime flower.

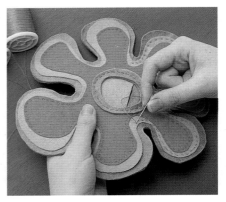

5 Cut out a ring of lilac felt to fit around the circle in the orange flower. Stitch it in place through all the layers using running stitch and a contrasting colour thread (floss). Work running stitches around the edge of the flowers in the same way. Insert the mirror through the slit in the back of the frame. Make a small buttonhole stitch loop to hang the frame.

We are surrounded by brightly coloured plastic containers, and they are a wonderful source of creative material. Make use of some recycled plastic to make this unusual and colourful mirror frame.

Plastic Fantastic

you will need
plastic laundry basket
junior hacksaw
pair of compasses
craft knife
several plastic bottles, lids and caps
pencil
scissors
glue gun
circular mirror

1 Cut off the base of a laundry basket using a junior hacksaw. With a pair of compasses, draw a circle in the middle of the base and cut it out.

2 Select a plastic lid and cut around the rim to make the inner frame for the mirror. Cut down the sides of the bottles and open out into flat sheets.

3 Draw flowers and leaves on to the plastic, using the templates provided, and cut out the shapes, using a pair of sharp scissors.

4 Use the craft knife to cut two lines down the middle of each leaf, and lift up the section to make a ridge. Glue the plastic shapes to the frame, using a glue gun. Glue the mirror in place.

5 Glue a bottle cap to the back of the frame, using the glue gun. You can slip the cap over a screw in the wall to hang up the frame.

The backed ragwork of this frame is stiff enough to hold the unorthodox shape even when it is hanging on the wall. The design has an uncut loop pile surface, and you can use any oddments of fabric to make it.

Rag Rug Frame

you will need

marker pen

ruler

cardboard, 50cm/20in square

scissors

hessian (burlap), at least
70cm/28in square

wooden frame

staple gun

assorted fabrics, in four colours

silver foil and crisp or sweet wrappers

rug hook

latex carpet adhesive and applicator

2 pieces of black felt: 50cm/20in
and 18cm/7in square

strong, clear glue

needle

matching thread

dressmaker's pins

ring pull, from a drinks (soda) can

picture glass, 15cm/6in square

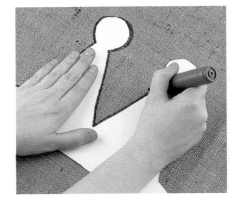

1 Draw the frame shape on cardboard. The shape is based on a 20cm/8in square with triangles and circles added. Cut out the shape, then cut out a 13cm/5in square in the centre. Place the template on the hessian (burlap) and draw round it.

2 Attach the hessian to a wooden frame, using a staple gun. Cut the fabric and foil into strips 1cm/½in wide. Start to hook the rags just beyond the central square. Outline all the shapes first. Take the fabric ends through to the top of the work.

3 Fill in the shapes, changing colours as desired. Leave the centres of the four circles to the end.

4 Fill in the centres of the circles with hooked foil strips, worked closely.

5 Remove the hessian from the frame, and place it on a flat surface. Cut around the shape, leaving a border at least 5cm/2in wide.

6 Apply a thin layer of latex adhesive over the back of the work, including the central picture area and the border. Leave to dry for 3–5 minutes. Fold in the outside border, then make diagonal cuts in the central picture area and fold back the pieces of hessian. Trim off any excess hessian. Leave to dry for 30 minutes.

7 Cut out the large piece of black felt to fit the shape of the frame. Apply dabs of strong, clear glue on the back of the work, and press on the felt. Carefully cut into the centre to reveal the picture area. Slipstitch the felt backing cloth to the back of the frame to attach it securely.

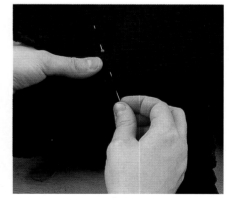

8 Use the remaining black felt to make a pocket. Pin in the centre of the back of the frame, then blanket stitch round three sides, leaving the top side open. Stitch the ring pull in position on the back of the frame, at the centre top. Slip the picture glass into the pocket.

Painting silk is easier than it might appear. If you place a template under the silk, it will show through the light coloured fabric. You can use metallic outliner to trace the lines of the template on to the silk.

Painted Silk Frame

❀❀❀

you will need

drawing paper

selection of coloured pencils

tracing paper

black felt-tipped pen

heavyweight habotai silk

iron

wooden silk-painting frame

silk pins

vanishing fabric marker pen

masking tape

metallic gutta and applicator

iron-fix (set) silk paints

artist's paintbrushes

paper tissue

2 sheets of clean white paper

scissors

spray adhesive

cardboard

1 Trace the design provided and work out the colours to co-ordinate with the picture to be framed. Then draw your final design on to tracing paper with a black felt-tipped pen.

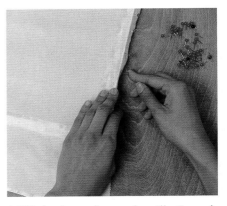

2 Wash, dry and iron the silk. Stretch it on to a wooden frame and hold it in position with silk pins. The fabric must be absolutely taut, without any wrinkles.

3 Using a vanishing fabric marker pen, trace the design on to the underside of the stretched silk, holding the tracing paper on the other side with pieces of masking tape at each corner.

4 Apply metallic gutta to the outline of the design. This will block the mesh of the silk, preventing the silk paints from bleeding and merging. Allow the gutta to dry.

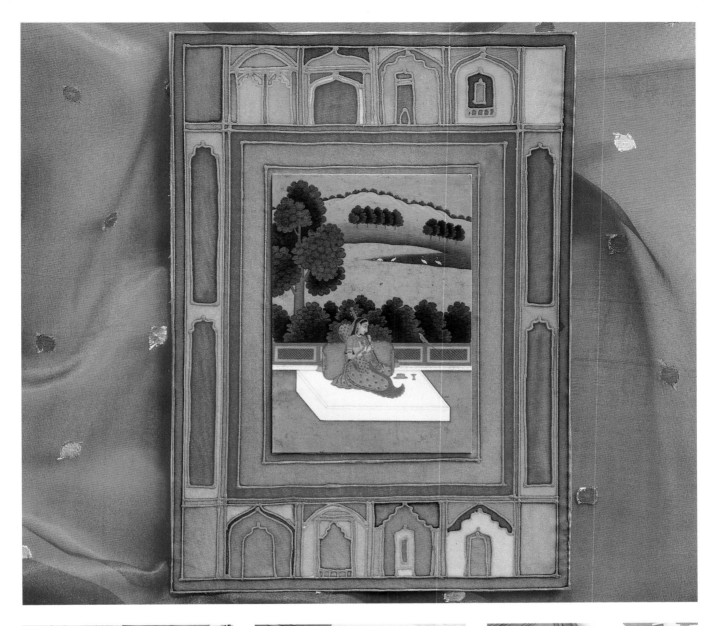

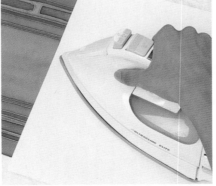

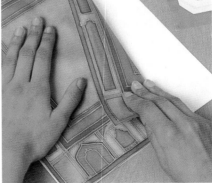

5 Following your initial sketch, apply silk paints to the design, taking care not to splash or go over any lines of gutta. Keep a tissue to hand to mop up any excess paint from your brush.

6 Place the silk between two sheets of clean white paper and iron it, according to the paint manufacturer's instructions, to fix the paint.

7 Cut neatly around the silk design. The gutta border will prevent the silk from fraying. Use spray adhesive to mount the silk on cardboard, and stick your picture in the centre.

Plaster, Clay
and Mosaic

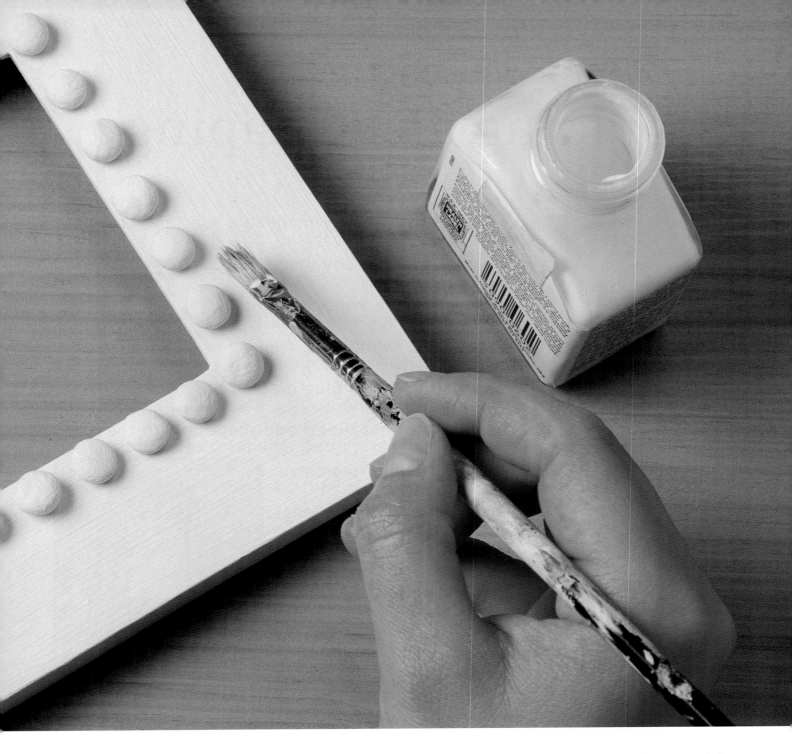

Working with clay and mosaic can be more challenging than working with other media, but the end results can be stunning. You can mould decorative motifs to glue on to a plain frame, or model the whole frame from clay. Choose from the wide variety of colours available or tint the clay yourself. Use mosaic tiles, smashed china, gemstones or mirror tiles to create a range of original and individual mosaic frames.

Plaster is rather fragile for a frame, unless it is very thick, but it can be moulded into lovely decorations for wooden frames. Modelling clay is more durable, and can be strengthened by baking or adding hardeners.

Plaster and Clay Materials

Modelling clay
There are many brands and qualities. Air-dried clay does not require firing.

Plaster
Modelling plaster is always added to the water to mix. Measure the amount of water needed by pouring it into the mould, sprinkle in dry plaster until it starts to mound up out of the water, then stir it in.

Polymer clay
This modelling plastic is available in many colours and special finishes such as fluorescent and metallic. It is hardened by baking at a low temperature in a domestic oven.

Shells
Embed small seashells in a clay frame or incorporate in mosaic.

Acrylic varnish
Used for protecting painted clay and plaster surfaces.

Glass nuggets and stones
Embed decorative stones and beads in clay frames. Use glass nuggets if they are to be baked with polymer clay.

Glue
PVA (white) glue can be used as a sealant. Two-part epoxy resin glue is very strong and can be used to join hardened polymer clay and to attach hanging fixtures.

Metal leaf
Use Dutch metal imitation gold or silver leaf or apply copper or aluminium leaf to clay or plaster for decoration.

Mirror tiles
These can be inserted into frames to make small mirrors, or broken and embedded in clay. Wear gloves and safety goggles when breaking glass.

Talcum powder
Sprinkle on boards and cutters to stop them sticking to the clay.

Wire
Embed a wire hook in the back of a clay frame while it is still soft.

Wood
Cut bases for plaster or clay frames from plywood or medium density fibreboard (MDF), or use planks from wooden fruit crates.

Moulds and modelling tools for plaster and clay work are available in many different shapes, but you can find much of what you need in the kitchen, and ordinary utensils may give you fresh ideas for designs.

Plaster and Clay Equipment

Modelling tools
A range of different shapes and sizes is useful for working with modelling and polymer clay.

Moulds
Specialist moulds are available for plaster, but you can also use containers such as baking tins or ice-cube trays.

Nail file or emery board
Used for filing hardened clay smooth before painting or sealing.

Nylon scouring pad
Used for smoothing rough plaster.

Petroleum jelly
For greasing plaster moulds to allow the hardened plaster to be removed.

Rolling guides
Place two strips of wood of equal depth on each side of a piece of clay and use as guides to roll the clay evenly.

Rolling pin and board
Use a domestic rolling pin for large pieces of clay and a small, cake decorator's rolling pin and non-stick board for small pieces.

Tissue blade
Designed for taking human tissue samples, this very sharp blade is used to cut thin slices from polymer clay.

Brayer
A small roller, like a printing ink roller, can be used to roll out very small pieces of clay, to smooth a clay surface or to rub over metal leaf to help it adhere.

Cocktail sticks (toothpicks)
Used to make very small holes in clay.

Drinking straws
The end of a plastic drinking straw can be used to cut out tiny circles in clay.

Found objects
Many different objects can be used to impress designs in soft clay.

Greaseproof (waxed) paper
Assemble polymer clay frames on greaseproof paper so that they can be moved to the oven for hardening.

Knives
Use a sharp kitchen knife or a craft knife to trim clay. Use a round-bladed knife to indent clay.

Working with modelling clay

Modelling clay can be sticky to work with. A light dusting of talcum powder on the work surface and on the rolling pin helps prevent the clay from sticking and distorting your designs.

Rolling out

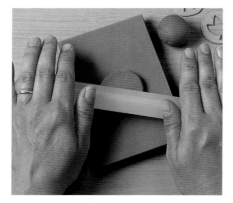

1 Work on a surface that can easily be wiped clean. Take enough clay to complete the section you are working on. Flatten the clay with your hands then roll with the pin. Turn the clay around and keep rolling until you have a smooth, even slab.

2 A small non-stick rolling board and rolling pin designed for cake decorating are especially useful for rolling out small pieces of clay for delicate work.

Embossing and moulding

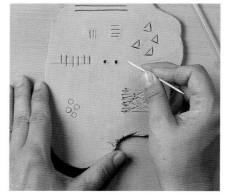

Before starting a project that requires surface decoration, practise on a spare piece of clay. Make small holes with a cocktail stick (toothpick), the rounded end of a knife, or by pressing a drinking straw into the clay and removing it with the plug of clay inside. Scratch the surface of the clay and emboss with found objects.

Cutting around a template

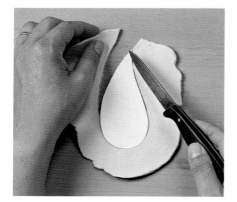

1 Some brands of modelling clay can be quite fibrous when cut, so neaten the edges with a modelling tool or the edge of a knife as you work. Moisten the tool slightly with water as needed.

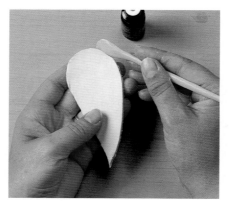

2 Smooth the edges with a modelling tool for a more rounded edge or use your fingertips, lightly moistened with hand cream.

Filing rough edges

When the work is dry, remove any rough edges with a nail file or emery board. Sand carefully, as dry clay can be powdery and is delicate. Use a nail file for reaching small areas and fine sandpaper for large surfaces. Seal with PVA (white) glue.

Working with mosaic

When embarking on your first mosaic, use a simple design, such as a geometric pattern, and concentrate on finding the right colour combinations. Often, this can produce the most effective mosaics.

1 Hold the material to be cut between the tips of the cutting edges of a pair of tile nippers. Squeeze the handles together, and the tesserae should break in two along the line of impact. Nippers are also useful for cutting tesserae into a specific shape.

2 When breaking up larger ceramics, such as tiles, and if regular shapes are not required, break the material with a hammer. When doing this, always wear a pair of goggles or cover the tile or china with a piece of sacking.

3 Mark the frame into small, equally spaced sections. Using a dark pencil or a marker pen, draw a simple motif in each section. Here, the motif is a daisy.

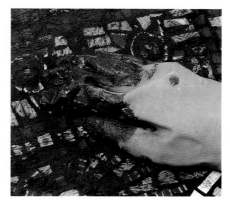

4 Mix up some cement-based tile adhesive and, working on a small area at a time, spread it along the lines of your drawing. Press the tesserae firmly into the cement. Choose shapes that echo those of the design, for example, the petal shapes of the flower. When each motif is tiled, thoroughly wipe off any excess cement with a sponge and leave to dry overnight.

5 Break up tiles in the background colour with a hammer. Working on a small area of the frame at a time, spread cement-based adhesive on to the unfilled sections and press the tesserae into it. When the surface is covered, use small pieces of the background colour to tile along the outer edges of the frame, ensuring that the tesserae do not overlap the edge. Leave to dry for 24 hours.

6 Mix powdered grout with water. If you wish the grout to have a colour, add cement dye, vinyl matt emulsion or acrylic paint to the mixture (for indoor use, cement dye is not essential). Wearing rubber (latex) gloves, spread the grout over the surface using a squeegee or a flexible knife. Rub the grout into the gaps with your fingers.

Made from self-hardening clay, the colours and diamond shape of this pretty mirror frame are reminiscent of a harlequin's costume. Each corner is embellished with glass nuggets and swirls of copper wire.

Harlequin Pattern Frame

you will need

copper wire

wire cutters

ruler

round-nosed (snub-nosed) pliers

pencil

scissors

cardboard

rolling pin

self-hardening clay

cutting mat

clay modelling tool

diamond-shaped mirror

4 glass nuggets

acrylic paints

paintbrushes

1 Cut four 30cm/12in lengths of copper wire using wire cutters. Twist both ends of each wire into spirals with round-nosed (snub-nosed) pliers.

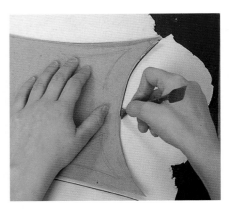

2 Enlarge the template provided at the back of the book and use this to cut a template out of cardboard. Roll out the clay to a thickness of about 5mm/¼in and cut it to shape using the template and a modelling tool on a cutting mat. Keep the tool wet all the time you are using it.

3 Centre the mirror on the clay and press down firmly to make a shallow indentation.

4 Remove the mirror. Score a diamond shape 1cm/½in inside the indentation and remove the centre.

5 Roll out a second piece of clay and cut around the mirror, leaving a 1cm/½in border all the way around. Replace the mirror in the centre of the frame. Centre the clay diamond on top of the mirror.

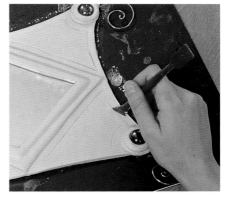

6 Wet your fingers and smooth down the overlap all around the mirror. Seal the edges with the modelling tool, so that the mirror is held securely between two layers of clay. Cut a diamond shape 1cm/½in in from the edges of the mirror and remove the piece of clay from the middle, revealing the mirror.

7 Make eight clay balls and place one in each corner of the frame. Working on one corner at a time, press on a ball to flatten it, place a wire on it and push a second ball on top, then add a glass nugget on top of that. Push hard so that all the pieces are firmly attached. Repeat in the other corners.

8 Score a pattern near the corners of the frame. Leave the frame to dry for 2–3 days and then paint it with acrylic paints.

Modelling plaster is readily available and easy to use. Look around for unusual cake tins or moulds in which to create plaster shapes. The red frame has been tinted using shoe polish as a quick colouring.

Plaster Cast Frame

you will need

springform ring cake tin (pan)
petroleum jelly
modelling plaster
bowl
jug (optional)
flexible plastic decorative ice cube tray
nylon scouring pad
soft cloth
coloured shoe polish
wooden frame, prepared and sanded
paintbrush
emulsion (latex) paint: white
strong glue
glue brush

1 Grease the inside of the cake tin (pan) with petroleum jelly. Assemble the tin and ensure it is watertight.

2 To make the plaster, add modelling plaster to a bowl of water until a mound of plaster forms out of the water. Mix the plaster with your hand.

3 Pour the plaster into the cake tin mould. (You may find it easier to use a jug.) When the tin is half full, pour the excess plaster into a decorative ice cube tray to make motifs for use on the second frame. Tap the moulds to remove any air bubbles from the bottom and sides.

4 After about 4–5 minutes, the plaster in the tin will begin to harden. Make an indentation around the centre, removing some of the plaster, to make a rebate for the picture.

5 When the plaster is completely hard, remove it from the mould and smooth off the sides and any rough edges with a nylon scouring pad.

6 Allow the plaster to dry thoroughly – this can take up to a week. With a soft cloth, apply a liberal coating of coloured shoe polish to colour and seal the plaster. The plaster will absorb some of the colour.

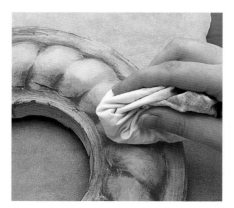

7 After about 10 minutes, rub off the shoe polish with the soft cloth, leaving traces of colour in the recesses.

8 To decorate a wooden frame, turn out the plaster shapes from the ice cube tray and smooth off the edges of the bases with the nylon scouring pad.

9 Paint the frame with white emulsion (latex) paint. When the paint is dry, glue on the plaster shapes. Allow the glue to dry completely.

These pure white frames are co-ordinated yet individually decorated. Restrained, geometric relief designs add interest with the play of light and shadow, yet do not overwhelm the contents of the frames.

Geometric Clay Frames

you will need

3mm/⅛in rolling guides

rolling pin

white modelling clay

small round and square metal cutters
(cookie cutters)

cocktail stick (toothpick)

round-ended knife

masking tape

acrylic or emulsion (latex) paint: white

paintbrushes

wooden frames, prepared and sanded

emery board

wood glue

matt acrylic varnish

1 Roll out a small piece of clay to an even thickness of about 3mm/⅛in. Using a round cutter, cut out several shapes from the clay.

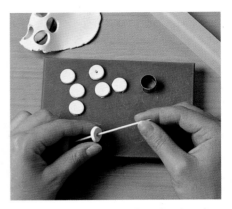

2 Pierce the centre of each clay disc with a cocktail stick (toothpick) and allow to dry.

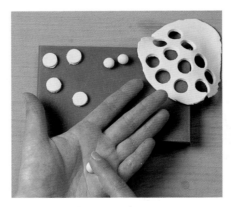

3 For an alternate design, cut out a number of clay discs as before. Roll each disc in the palm of your hand, then between your fingers to make a number of evenly sized balls. Allow the balls to dry thoroughly.

4 Roll out more clay and cut out small squares using a square cutter. Decorate the squares with different marks using the flat end of a knife. Aim to have about five different designs. Stick each to a flat surface with masking tape so that the edges do not curl. Allow to dry completely.

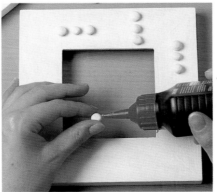

5 Apply several coats of white acrylic or emulsion (latex) paint to the frames, allowing each coat to dry before applying the next.

6 File any rough edges from the clay motifs using an emery board. When you are satisfied with the arrangement stick each in place with wood glue.

7 When the glue is dry, apply one or two coats of white paint to the entire frame, followed by several coats of matt acrylic varnish. Allow each coat to dry before applying the next.

Whether you want to jot down reminders for yourself or to leave important messages for somebody else, this little chalkboard in its rustic frame is perfect for the potting shed or to hang on the kitchen wall.

Modelled Flower Garden Frame

you will need

wooden fruit crate

saw

small chalkboard

mitre box

wood glue

staple gun

paintbrush

acrylic paints in a variety of colours

glue gun

modelling clay

modelling tools

rolling pin

sharp knife

tracing paper

pencil

scissors

medium artist's paintbrush

1 Remove the sides of the fruit crate and from it cut four lengths to fit the dimensions of the board. Mitre the corners. Use wood glue, then a staple gun, to hold the joints firmly. Paint the front of the frame green. Allow to dry. Glue the chalkboard to the back of the frame.

2 To model a flower, roll six balls of clay the same size. Put one ball aside until step 3. Squeeze the remaining five into a point at one end. Using a rounded modelling tool, press each into a fat petal. Arrange the petals into a flower shape.

3 Place the last ball in the flower centre and indent with a rounded modelling tool. For the fence, roll out the clay and cut two strips each 1cm/½in wide to fit across the frame. Cut short strips for the posts. Trim the top of each post to a point.

4 For the leaves, roll out the clay, then cut basic leaf shapes and smooth out the edges with your fingers. Use a pointed modelling tool to trace a central vein on each one. Make 12 leaves.

5 Trace the templates provided for the pot and watering can and cut out. Cut out the shapes from clay, using the templates as a guide. Smooth the clay edges with your fingers.

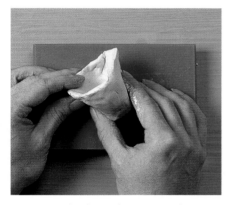

6 For each three-dimensional pot at the bottom of the chalkboard, roll a ball of clay in your hand, then model it into a small pot shape. Let all the clay pieces dry for a few days.

7 Using an artist's paintbrush, paint the shapes with acrylic paints in bright colours, and allow to dry.

8 Use a glue gun to attach the picket fence and the other decorations to the chalkboard frame.

Small decorated mirror frames are always appealing and this one is easy and fun to make. The colourful, bright-eyed lizards would be an ideal decoration for a child's bedroom with an animal theme.

Modelled Lizard Mirror Frame

you will need

1 block light turquoise polymer clay

brayer (small roller)

craft knife

round mirror, 13.5cm/5¼in diameter

½ block fluorescent pink and ¼ block magenta polymer clay, mixed 2:1

3 blocks dark turquoise polymer clay

small amounts polymer clay: grey, black and white

smoothing tool

D-ring

epoxy resin glue

1 Roll out the light turquoise clay to about 5mm/¼in thick. Cut five curved strips using the template at the back of the book and place them carefully around the edge of the mirror.

2 From the mixed pink and magenta clay, roll out two long sausages, one slightly thicker than the other. Use the thinner sausage to edge the inner ring of the border, and the thicker sausage to edge the outer ring.

3 Make the lizards from dark turquoise clay. For the legs, roll short sausages, flatten one end and bend for the knee and foot joints. Make 20.

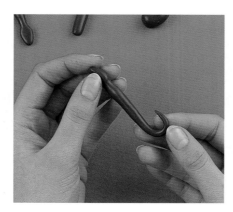

4 For each body, roll a tapered sausage from a piece of dark turquoise clay. Create a neck in the thicker end by rolling between your two index fingers and flatten out the head. Make four more bodies.

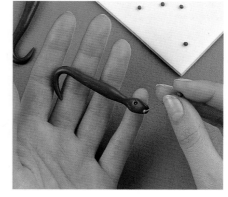

5 Roll tiny beads from grey, black and white clay for the eyes. Position the grey first and flatten, then add the black and finally the white on top. ▶

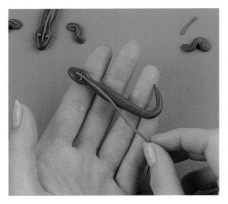

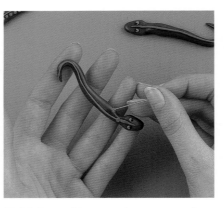

6 Roll thin strands of light turquoise clay to make a stripe for each lizard's back and its legs.

7 Make a thin tapering sausage from the pink clay and slice thinly to make subtly graded discs. Make approximately 18 per lizard. Roll the discs into balls, flatten and apply to either side of the back stripe.

8 Position the legs at equal intervals on the mirror surround so that all the front legs cover up the joins in the border. Press them into position using a smoothing tool.

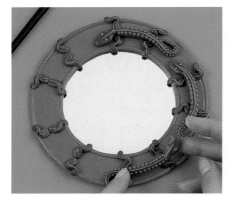

9 Place the lizards' bodies on top of the legs, carefully but firmly enough to ensure that they join properly. Bake for three-quarters of the manufacturer's recommended baking time.

10 Form another, thicker pink sausage and flatten it into a flat circle using the brayer (small roller). Press it in position around the back of the mirror edge, making sure that it adheres well.

11 Roll out a thin sheet of pink clay and make a semi-circle to fit within the back surround. Bake the mirror frame for the remainder of the recommended cooking time.

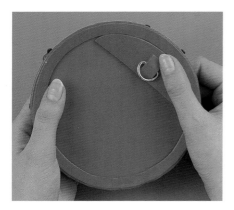

◄ **12** To position the D-ring for hanging, loop a thin strip of clay through the ring and make an indentation on the semi-circle but do not attach it yet. Remove the strip and the semi-circle and bake separately on a flat surface. When cool, glue the shape to the back of the mirror then add the tab, ensuring that the D-ring can move freely.

This mirror looks as if it might belong to a mermaid. The magical effect is achieved by encasing the mirror between two layers of polymer clay which have been covered with stretched copper leaf.

Starburst Clay Mirror

you will need

large block black polymer clay

brayer (small roller)

copper leaf

round mirror

craft knife

modelling tool

4 small blue glass cabochon stones

wire

3 large gemstones

acrylic paint: mauve, coral, blue and white

paintbrush

1 Roll out a 5mm/¼in thick sheet of polymer clay, about 3cm/1½in larger all round than the mirror. Apply copper leaf and crackle the surface (see Techniques). Press the mirror into the centre of the clay to embed it firmly.

2 Cut two rectangular pieces of clay to form the base of the handle. Press one into the edge of the mirror base. Prepare the second piece with crackled copper leaf as in step 1 and set it aside for use in step 8.

3 Prepare a thin strip of clay with copper leaf, rolled a little more thinly to give a finer crackle. Press it on to the clay base to surround the mirror.

4 Cut out three triangular pieces of clay. Cut off one of the points on each to form the three points of the cross. Apply copper leaf and crackle as in step 3, then press in place.

5 Using a modelling tool, press all round the inner and outer edges of the mirror surround to neaten them and to secure the mirror. Do the same around the cross points. ▶

6 Place a small cabochon stone on the mirror surround opposite each cross point and the handle. Score the cross points outwards to create a ray-like pattern.

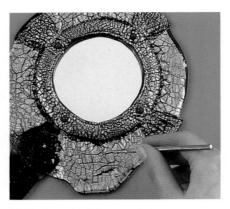

7 Etch a double-tiered zigzag pattern radiating out from the mirror surround to give a sunburst effect.

8 Bend a piece of wire into a hook at one end. Embed it along the length of the handle with the hook towards the mirror. Cover with the second part of the handle prepared in step 2, pressing the edges together.

9 Carefully mould the zigzag sunburst pattern around the mirror surround to create a staggered ray effect, then cut off the excess clay using a craft knife.

10 Press the large gemstones along the handle and delineate round them using the modelling tool.

11 Roll out a thin piece of clay and apply copper leaf to it. Cut it into three narrow strips and surround each gemstone with one. Press a pattern into the strips to secure the stones in position. Bake following the manufacturer's instructions.

◀ **12** Highlight the details with different coloured paints: variegated mauve on the outer spikes; variegated coral on the inner spikes; and variegated blue on the cross points and down the handle.

This recipe will make eight to ten frames. The colours are built up in blocks, from which you take slices for each frame. To make one frame, cut out all the basic shapes from 2mm/¹⁄₁₆in thick sheets of green clay.

Stitched Clay Frame

you will need

polymer clay: 2 blocks green, large block black, 2 blocks blue

tissue blade

smooth paper

small roller

craft knife

needle

greaseproof (waxed) paper

embroidery thread (floss): blue and yellow

corrugated or thick cardboard

knitting needle

jewellery head pins and pliers

epoxy resin glue

1 To make the roof, mould half a block of green clay into a triangular wedge. Cover with a thin skin of black clay. Then cover two sides with a thick blue layer and one side with black. Surround the whole with a thin layer of black. Using the tissue blade, trim the end of the wedge, then take off a thick slice across the wedge. Place a sheet of smooth paper over this and roll the slice to the required size.

2 Make a long oblong block in green clay, about 16 x 2.5 x 3cm/6½ x 1 x 1¼in. Surround it with a thin skin of black clay. Place a thick blue strip along the bottom. Cover the top with black for two-thirds of the length and with blue for the remainder, and finally with a thin layer of black. Make two smaller oblongs, about 6 x 2 x 3cm/2½ x ¾ x 1¼in, one of black, the other of green. Slice both in half then cut diagonally across each to make triangles.

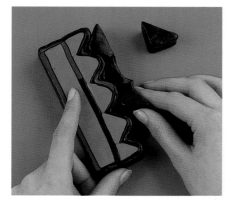

3 Centre three green triangles on the oblong block. Cut the last one in half and place at each end. Wrap the entire structure with thin black clay. Cover one side and halfway along the ridges with a thick blue layer and the remainder with a thick black layer. Add a thin black layer over the blue right down the opposite side.

◄ **4** Insert the black triangles between the green ones and compress the whole assembly, without distorting any of it, to pack all the elements together. Using the tissue blade, take off a thin 3mm/⅛in slice. Place a sheet of smooth paper over this and roll smooth. Cut out the black triangles with a craft knife, leaving a black edging. This will be the base. ►

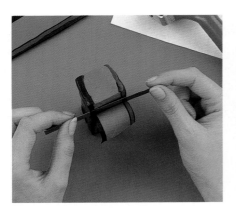

5 Make up another block, like the base block in step 2, but wider, about 16 × 4 × 3cm/6½ × 1½ × 1¼ in. Using the tissue blade, take off two thin 3mm/⅛ in slices the length of the oblong. Place a sheet of smooth paper over each and roll them smooth. These will be the sides.

6 Decorate the roof and sides. Make an oval cane of blue wrapped in black and cut three slices for the roof. Make long, thin blue and black sausages to make scroll patterns on the roof and sides. Cut tiny discs from the sausages to make spots.

7 Assemble the frame, securing the pieces with small pieces of black clay pressed across the joins at the back. Referring to the finished template for guidance, use a needle to make stitching holes. Add more spots to balance the design if you like. Cover the back with a thin layer of black clay, cutting out the window. Place the frame, face up, on a sheet of greaseproof (waxed) paper and bake following the manufacturer's instructions.

8 Stitch through the prepared holes with thread (floss), referring to the finished illustration. Roll out a 3mm/⅛ in thick black rectangle, slightly larger than the window. Place it over a sheet of corrugated cardboard or other thick cardboard and press all round it to create a pocket. Pierce a hole near the top using a knitting needle and reinforce it with a ring of clay.

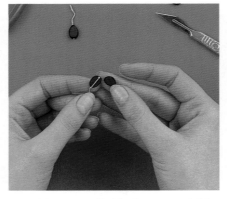

9 Make a small black-wrapped blue cane, press it into an egg shape and cut six slices. Sandwich a jewellery head pin between a pair of slices and kink the wire with pliers. Bake these with the pocket following the manufacturer's instructions.

10 Glue the pocket into position, pressing along the seams to ensure a good join. The gap should be wide enough to slide in a piece of glass and a picture. Glue the jewellery wire shapes in place.

Decorated with delicately patterned china in cool, fresh colours and with touches of gold, this attractive frame will add interest and atmosphere to a bathroom.

Arched Mosaic Mirror

you will need

plywood, 2cm/¾in thick

pencil

ruler

jigsaw

sandpaper (glasspaper)

PVA (white) glue

paintbrushes

wood primer

white undercoat

gloss paint

mirror plate

drill with rebating bit

2 screws, 2cm/¾in long

screwdriver

thick cardboard

scissors

mirror, 4mm/⅛in thick, cut to size

tile cement

flexible knife

masking tape

tracing paper (optional)

tile nippers

selection of china

powdered tile grout

vinyl matt emulsion (latex) or acrylic paint (optional)

mixing container

grout spreader or rubber (latex) gloves

stiff-bristled nailbrush

soft cloth

1 Draw the outer shape of the mirror frame on to a piece of plywood using the template provided. Cut out this shape using a jigsaw, then sand down the rough edges. On to this base panel, draw the shape of the mirror glass. Make sure it is a shape that glass-cutters will be able to reproduce.

2 Seal the sides and front of the base panel with diluted PVA (white) glue and paint the back first with wood primer, then undercoat and finally gloss paint. Mark the position of the mirror plate on the back of the panel. Using an appropriate bit, rebate the area that will be under the keyhole-shaped opening of the mirror plate (large enough to take a screw head). Then screw the plate into position.

3 Make a cardboard template to the exact dimensions of the mirror shape you have drawn on the base. Ask your supplier to cut a piece of foil-backed mirror matching your template.

4 Stick the mirror in position using ready-mixed tile cement. Leave to dry overnight. ▶

Small mosaic tiles make an attractive Mediterranean-style frame. To keep the project simple, plan the dimensions of the frame to suit the size of the tiles, to avoid having to cut and fit odd-shaped pieces.

Mediterranean Mirror

you will need

pencil

metal ruler

medium density fibreboard (MDF), 18mm/¾in thick

saw

drill

jigsaw

wood glue

white acrylic primer

paintbrush

tile cement

fine notched spreader

glass mosaic tiles

grout

soft cloth

mirror

narrow frame moulding

2 ring screws

brass picture wire

1 Draw a frame on MDF. Cut it out using a saw. Drill corner holes for the centre and cut this out with a jigsaw. Cut out a shelf and glue to the frame with wood glue. Allow to dry.

2 Prime both sides of the frame and shelf with white acrylic primer to seal it. Allow to dry. Apply tile cement to a small area of the frame, using a fine notched spreader.

3 Apply a random selection of tiles, leaving a 2mm/¹⁄₁₆in gap between each tile. Continue over the rest of the frame, working on a small area at a time. Tile the edges of the frame with a single row of tiles.

4 Allow to dry following the tile cement manufacturer's instructions. Spread grout over the surface of the tiles. Scrape off the excess.

5 Clean off any remaining grout with a soft cloth. Leave to dry thoroughly.

6 Place the mirror glass face down on the back of the frame and secure it with narrow frame moulding, glued in place with wood glue. Allow to dry.

7 Screw two ring screws in place on the back of the mirror, and tie on picture wire to hang the frame.

In this lovely hallway mirror, romantic red hearts and scrolling white lines are beautifully offset by the rich blue background, which sparkles with chunks of randomly placed mirror glass.

Valentine Mirror

1 Prime both sides of the plywood with diluted PVA (white) glue and leave to dry. Score the front with a sharp implement. Screw the mirror plate to the back of the plywood.

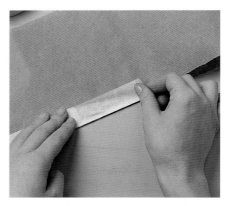

2 Cover the mirror glass with brown paper and tape it in place to protect the glass. Centre the mirror on the plywood and stick it in place using tile cement. Allow to dry.

3 Draw a small heart in the centre of each border and scrolling lines to connect the four hearts. Use the template at the back of the book if desired.

4 Using tile nippers and wearing goggles, cut the blue and red tiles into small, irregular pieces. Cut the white tiles into regular-sized squares.

5 Wearing rubber (latex) gloves, spread the tile cement over the hearts and press in the red tiles. Repeat for the white lines. Scrape off any excess cement and leave to dry.

6 Using a hammer and wearing goggles and gloves, break the blue and mirror tiles. Wrap each tile in a piece of heavy cloth before breaking it.

7 Spread tile cement over the background, then press in the tiles. Leave to dry. Grout the mosaic with cement, wearing rubber gloves as before and using a notched spreader.

8 Wearing a dust mask, carefully sand off any lumps of remaining cement which may have dried on the surface of the mosaic, using fine-grade sandpaper (glasspaper).

9 For a professional finish, rub tile cement into the back of the plywood board. Remove the protective brown paper from the mirror.

It is hard to believe that this beautiful, shell-encrusted frame started life as a plain wooden one. Texture is built up using neutral-coloured shells, such as limpets and cockles, embedded into tile cement.

Grotto Frame

you will need

assorted shells in neutral colours

wooden frame, prepared and sanded

white tile cement

small palette knife

PVA (white) glue and brush

blue limpet shells

small coloured shells

frosted glass beads

tweezers

small clear glass beads in 3 toning colours

large matchstick

emulsion (latex) paint: white

paintbrush

1 Attach the shells to the frame using white tile cement and a small palette knife. Allow the shells to overlap the edges at the top and sides of the frame to disguise its square shape and to create a grotto-like effect.

2 Continue to cover the frame around the inside edge, allowing the shells to overlap the edge as before.

3 Fill in the gaps between the shells with smaller shells.

4 Select knobbly shells to cover the side and top edges of the frame; attach them with cement as before. Leave to dry for several hours.

5 Use PVA (white) glue to stick on decorative blue limpets and small coloured shells.

6 To add colour and texture, glue on frosted glass beads, using tweezers to position them.

7 Mix the clear glass beads into some glue. Using a large matchstick, add blobs of this mixture in the gaps between the shells on the frame. Leave the glue to dry.

8 Paint the back of the frame white. If the frame is free-standing, it is important that the back looks attractive, so finish by attaching a few more shells to the top of the frame.

Semi-precious stones, such as agate and carnelian, can be found on some beaches. To identify them, hold them up to the light and they will glow with shades of warm ochre or deep russet.

Rock Pool Mirror

you will need
paper
pencil
metal ruler
scissors
craft knife
cutting mat
polyboard
pair of compasses
bradawl (awl)
wire
PVA (white) glue and brush
circular mirror glass, 10cm/4in diameter
masking tape
small sticks
tile cement
small palette knife or spreader
small pebbles
semi-precious stones
aquarium gravel
watercolour paints
small artist's paintbrush
palette

1 Draw a hexagon template on a piece of paper. Using a craft knife and metal ruler and working on a cutting mat, cut two hexagons from polyboard. Draw a circle 9.5cm/3¾in in diameter in the centre of one of the pieces.

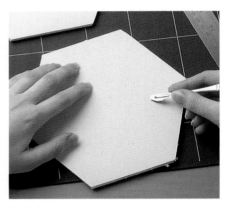

2 Cut out the circle with a craft knife, holding the knife at an angle so that the hole has a sloping edge. Keep the cut-out circle.

3 Using a bradawl (awl), pierce two holes in the hexagon. Thread the wire loop through the holes for hanging the mirror and twist the ends shut.

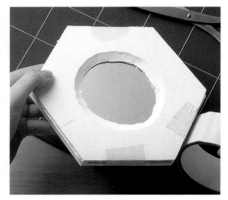

4 Glue the mirror glass in the centre of the backing, with the wire loop on the back. Place the other hexagon right side up on top to form a sandwich, and tape together.

5 Cut sticks to fit along the edges of the frame, overlapping them at the corners. Glue in place. Leave to dry.

6 Replace the cut-out circle to protect the glass. Spread tile cement over the frame, then arrange the pebbles and semi-precious stones on top, lightly pressing them into the cement. Leave the frame to dry.

7 Remove the polyboard circle. Mix the aquarium gravel with PVA (white) glue and fill in the gaps between the stones, especially around the inner edge. Leave to dry. Add a second layer of sticks to the outside edge. Mix watercolour paint with plenty of water and wash over the grout to blend it in.

Templates

Enlarge the templates on a photocopier. Alternatively, trace the design and draw a grid of evenly spaced squares over your tracing. Draw a larger grid on to another piece of paper and copy the outline square by square. Finally, draw over the lines to make sure they are continuous.

Painted vine mirror frame, p92

Leaf-stippled frames, p81

Framed chalkboard, p84–85

Raised motif frame, p82–83

Starry cardboard frame, p133

Batik frame, p119–121

Seaside papier mâché
mirror, p134

Egg carton frame,
p146–147

Repoussé frame, p148

Swirly mirror,
p140–141

Punched tin leaf frame,
p154–155

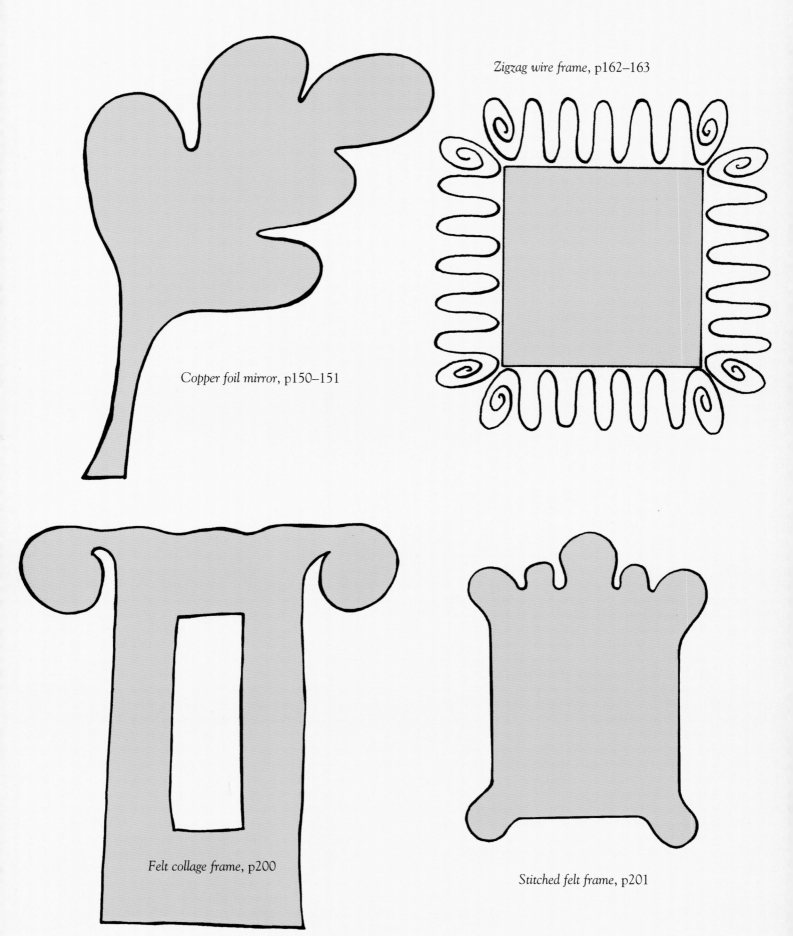

Copper foil mirror, p150–151

Zigzag wire frame, p162–163

Felt collage frame, p200

Stitched felt frame, p201

Painted silk frame, p208–209

Fun felt frame,
p202–203

Rag rug frame, p206–207

Plastic fantastic,
p204–205

Harlequin pattern frame, p220–221

Arched mosaic mirror, p237–239

Stitched clay frame, p234–236

Valentine mirror, p242–243

Modelled flower garden frame, p226–227

Modelled lizard mirror frame, p228–230

Index

Acknowledgements

The publisher would like to thank the following people for designing projects in this book:

Helen Baird for the Valentine Mirror pp242–243.
Deena Beverley for the Twine Picture Frame pp184–185.
Petra Boase for the Leaf-stipple Frames p81, Bead-encrusted Frames pp188–189.
Penny Boylan for the Country-style Noticeboard pp180–181, Geometric Picture Frames pp224–225.
Victoria Brown for Using Decorative Mouldings pp36–37, Poppy Seedhead Frames pp178–179, String Spirals Frame pp186–187, Stitched Felt Frame p201, Fun Felt Frame pp202–203, Plastic Fantastic pp204–205, Plaster Cast Frame pp222–223, Mediterranean Mirror pp240–241.
Sandy Bryant for the Ivy Leaf Frame pp144–145.
Elizabeth Couzins-Scott for the Hammered Paper Frame p135.
Ann Dyson for the Modelled Lizard Mirror Frame pp228–230.
Marion Elliot for the Starry Cardboard Frame p133, Seaside Papier Mâché Mirror p134, Celtic Jewelled Frame p149, Painted Tinware Mirror pp160–161.
Tessa Evelegh for the Aromatic Picture Frame p176.
Lucinda Ganderton for the Padded Silk Picture Frame pp194–195.
Sandra Hadfield for the Swirly Mirror pp140–141.
Stephanie Harvey for the Restoration Frame pp98–99.
Alison Jenkins for the Pressed Flowerhead pp101–103, Zigzag Wire Frame pp162–163, Modelled Flower Garden Frame pp226–227.
Rian Kanduth for the Single Window Mount p15, Multiple Window Frame pp16–17, Stepped Mount pp18–19, Fabric-covered Mount pp20–21, Decorating a Mount: Marbled Border p24, Multi-window Frame pp46–47, Reclaimed Timber Frame pp50–51, Framing a Canvas pp54–55, Insetting

Objects into a Frame pp56–57, Framing an Engraved Stone p58, Decorative Lettering p59, Cutting Glass p61, Colourwashed Frame pp78–79, Raised Motif Frame pp82–83, Oil-gilded Frame pp96–97, Lime-waxed Frame p90, Woodstained Frame pp91, Craquelure Frame p106, Verre Eglomisé Mirror pp107–109, Ink Penwork Frame pp112–113, Scorched Frame pp114–115, Tortoiseshell Frame pp116–118, Decoupage Frame pp142–143, Lead Frame pp152–153, Metal Foil Frame pp158–159.
Dinah Kelly for the Crackle-glaze Picture Frame pp104–105.
Kitchen Table Studios for the Starburst Mirror pp231–233.
Mary Maguire for the Repoussé Frame p148, Wire Picture Frame pp156–157, Rustic Picture Frame p183, Stitched Clay Frame pp234–236, Grotto Frame pp244–245, Rock Pool Mirror pp246–247.
Cleo Mussi for the Arched Mosaic Mirror pp237–239.
Penny Plouviez for the Copper Foil Mirror pp150–151.
Maggie Pryce for the Gilded Mirror pp136–137.
Lizzie Reakes for the Rag Rug Frame pp206–207.
Andrea Spencer for the Corrugated Picture Frame p132.
Karen Spurgin for the Sequins and Beads pp190–191.
Isabel Stanley for the Flowered Frame pp192–193.
Susie Stokoe for the Batik Frame pp119–121, Gold Leaf Picture Frame pp208–209.
Michael Savage for the Punched Tin Leaf Frame pp154–155.
Liz Wagstaff for the Gilded Shell Frame pp86–87, Good as Gold pp94–95, Water-gilded Frame pp110–111.
Stewart Walton for the Stamped Star Frame p80, Framed Chalkboard pp84–85, Egg Carton Frame pp146–147, Bottle Cap Mirror Frame pp164–165.
Dorothy Wood for The Parts of the Frame p14, Shaped Mounts pp22–23,

Decorating a Frame: Decorative lines p25, Colourwashing p25, Sponging p26, Choosing Mount Sizes p27, Securing the Artwork pp28–29, Mouldings pp30–31, Cutting and Joining a Basic Frame pp32–33, Creating a Rebate pp34–35, Hexagonal Frame p38–39, Halving Joint Frame p40–41, Cross-over Frame pp42–43, Jigsaw Puzzle Frame pp44–45, Choosing Glass p60, Fitting up a Frame pp62–63, Adding Fillets p64, Hanging Pictures p65, Oranges and Lemons Decoupage pp138–139, Ribbonwork Frame pp198–199.

Thanks to the following for individual projects: Ofer Acoo, Deborah Alexander, Michael Ball, Amanda Blunden, Esther Burt, Gill Clement, Louise Gardam, Jill and David Hancock, Rachel Howard Marshall, Terry Moore, Jack Moxley; Oliver Moxley, Deborah Schneebeli-Morrell, Debbie Siniska, Karen Triffitt and Josephine Whitfield.

Thanks to the following photographers: Steve Dalton, Nicki Dowey, Rodney Forte, Michelle Garrett, Rose Jones, Debbie Patterson, Spike Powell, Graham Rae, Steve Tanner, Adrian Taylor, Lucy Tizard, Peter Williams and Polly Wreford.